Wilkinson's Road '

Referenuu

2008

By

Her Honour Judge Katharine Marshall (Editor)

MA (Cantab), Circuit Judge

and

Peter Wallis (Consultant Editor)

MA (Oxon), District Judge (Magistrates' Courts),
Recorder of the Crown Court

LONDON
SWEET & MAXWELL
2008

Published in 2008 by
Sweet & Maxwell Limited of 100 Avenue Road,
http://www.sweetandmaxwell.co.uk
Typeset by LBJ Typesetting Ltd of Kingsclere
Printed and bound in Great Britain by
Athenaeum Press Ltd, Gateshead

No natural forests were destroyed to make this product;
only farmed timber was used and re-planted.

British Library Cataloguing in Publication Data

A CIP catalogue record for this book
is available from the British Library

ISBN 978-1-847-03510-3

Preface

Welcome to the second edition of Wilkinson's Road Traffic Referencer. Following the success of the first edition, the Referencer has been brought up to date to take account of changes that have occurred over the last year. The law is up to date as at April 30, 2008, and where changes are anticipated to come into effect in the near future, these are included.

The A–Z format is continued to allow practitioners to find the relevant information quickly. For each offence covered, the statutory provisions are set out together with short commentary, case references and applicable sentencing guidelines. The appendices contain extensive extracts from the schedules to the Road Traffic Offenders Act 1988. I have aimed to include as much information as possible to avoid the need to access other books or reference works when dealing with the majority of road traffic offences suitable to be dealt with as summary offences. More obscure offences or particularly specialist points may need to be researched in more depth. To assist, the Referencer gives the relevant chapter in the main *Wilkinson* publication. The Referencer also covers current practice and procedure and sets out how cases are likely to be dealt with in the magistrates' court, identifying good practice. Changes brought in by the Road Safety Act 2006, including in relation to alternative verdicts, the introduction of a statutory definition of careless driving and changes in penalties for some offences, have all been included.

The Referencer continues to contain extensive coverage of offences relating to drink-driving as these make up a considerable percentage of the cases in court lists. The 2008 edition has included the most relevant recent case law, including clarification of what constitutes "expertise" allowing opinion evidence to be admitted, and also covers in some detail the testing regime now in place (preliminary and evidential test provisions).

Also covered in detail are provisions relating to endorsement and disqualification, with clear distinctions being drawn between the different orders available and the circumstances when the court must impose such orders and when it remains a matter of discretion. The DVLA table of endorsable offence codes and the number of points that may be imposed is also included.

The Highway Code has been updated since the first edition of the Referencer. This edition provides an online reference to the full document, and contains useful extracts on speed limits and stopping distances.

The most significant change to this edition is the inclusion of the up-to-date sentencing guidelines which will replace the current guidelines contained in the first edition. These are expected to come into effect in October 2008 and, as they are to be issued by the Sentencing Guidelines Council, will be binding on sentencers unless there is a good reason to depart from them. Practitioners will want to be fully up to date with the new guidance and to be aware of the factors that are likely to feature in decision-making so that they may address the court with information on the relevant issues. Although not in force until later in the year, it was felt sensible to include them in this edition to ensure that it remains a useful tool until the next edition. However, until the guidelines take effect, practitioners are invited to keep to hand the first edition and refer to the magistrates' court guidelines therein.

I hope that you will find somewhere in this small book the information you need to know and that the Referencer proves as useful as I intended it should be.

Katharine Marshall

To all road users—Think Bike

Contents

Part 2—Appendices

Table of Cases

Table of Statutes

Table of Statutory Instruments

Part 1:

Road Traffic Referencer

Accident, Duty of driver to stop, report accident and give information or show documents

(Reference: Wilkinson's Road Traffic Offences, Ch.7.)

The duties of a driver, when a road traffic accident has occurred, are set out in s.170 of the Road Traffic Act 1988 as follows:

170 DUTY OF DRIVER TO STOP, REPORT ACCIDENT AND GIVE INFORMATION OR PRODUCE DOCUMENTS

(1) This section applies in a case where, owing to the presence of a mechanically propelled vehicle on a road or other public place,[1] an accident occurs by which—

    (a) personal injury is caused to a person other than the driver of that mechanically propelled vehicle, or

    (b) damage is caused—

        (i) to a vehicle other than that mechanically propelled vehicle or a trailer drawn by that mechanically propelled vehicle, or

        (ii) to an animal other than an animal in or on that mechanically propelled vehicle or a trailer drawn by that mechanically propelled vehicle, or

        (iii) to any other property constructed on, fixed to, growing in or otherwise forming part of the land on which the road or place in question is situated or land adjacent to such land.

(2) The driver of the mechanically propelled vehicle must stop and, if required to do so by any person having reasonable grounds for so requiring, give his name and address and also the name and address of the owner and the identification marks of the vehicle.

(3) If for any reason the driver of the mechanically propelled vehicle does not give his name and address under subsection (2) above, he must report the accident.

(4) A person who fails to comply with subsection (2) or (3) above is guilty of an offence.

(5) If, in a case where this section applies by virtue of subsection (1)(a) above, the driver of a motor vehicle[2] does not at the time of the

---

[1] An amendment introduced by the Motor Vehicles (Compulsory Insurance) Regulations 2000 reg.2(6) extended this section to cover vehicles on public places, in addition to roads.

[2] Note that the duty to produce documents only arises in relation to a motor vehicle.

accident produce such a certificate of insurance or security, or other evidence, as is mentioned in section 165(2)(a) of this Act—

(a) to a constable, or

(b) to some person who, having reasonable grounds for so doing, has required him to produce it,

the driver must report the accident and produce such a certificate or other evidence.

This subsection does not apply to the driver of an invalid carriage.

(6) To comply with a duty under this section to report an accident or to produce such a certificate of insurance or security, or other evidence, as is mentioned in section 165(2)(a) of this Act, the driver—

(a) must do so at a police station or to a constable, and

(b) must do so as soon as is reasonably practicable and, in any case, within twenty-four hours of the occurrence of the accident.

(7) A person who fails to comply with a duty under subsection (5) above is guilty of an offence, but he shall not be convicted by reason only of a failure to produce a certificate or other evidence if, within seven days after the occurrence of the accident, the certificate or other evidence is produced at a police station that was specified by him at the time when the accident was reported.

(8) In this section "animal" means horse, cattle, ass, mule, sheep, pig, goat or dog.

A driver[3] must stop his vehicle if there has been an accident owing to the presence of his vehicle on a road or other public place,[4] in which either personal injury is caused to someone other than the driver of that vehicle, or damage is caused to another vehicle[5] or to an animal (except an animal in the driver's vehicle) or to any property attached to the road or land adjacent to it. Where the only injury, or damage, is to the driver or his vehicle (or animal in his vehicle), no duties arise. However, the section applies where injury is caused to a passenger in the driver's vehicle.

If required to by someone who has reasonable grounds for so requiring, the driver must give:

i) his own name and address[6];

ii) the name and address of the owner of the vehicle;

iii) the identification marks of the vehicle.

---

[3] It is the driver who has duties under s.170, not the owner or anyone else.

[4] The obligation arises regardless of who may be "at fault" in causing the accident.

[5] The vehicle damaged need not be a mechanically propelled vehicle.

[6] The address must be one through which the driver can be contacted and need not be his home address. See *DPP v McCarthy* [1999] R.T.R. 323.

If the driver fails to provide his name and address, he must report the accident at a police station or to a constable as soon as is reasonably practicable and within 24 hours of the accident.[7]

The driver must be aware that an accident has occurred,[8] and it will be a defence for a driver to prove absence of knowledge. As there is no statutory requirement on the prosecution to prove knowledge, once damage or injury has been established, the burden of proving lack of knowledge falls on the defence, on the balance of probabilities. Knowledge will be established where a driver really knows that there has been an accident but deliberately chooses to put it out of his mind.

The duty to stop arises immediately when and where the accident occurs. Stopping a distance down the road will not suffice.[9]

"Stop" means stop and remain at the scene of the accident for long enough[10] to enable interested parties to require of the driver directly[11] the information which might be required under the section.[12] The driver should remain near the vehicle,[13] but does not have to wait indefinitely.[14] There is no duty to actively seek out interested persons who might wish to have the relevant information.[15]

There is no statutory definition of "accident" as it applies to s.170. It appears one should look at the ordinary meaning of the word and apply common sense: "would an ordinary man in the circumstances of the case say there had been an accident?" The fact of a deliberate act does not preclude an occurrence from being an accident, nor need there be another vehicle involved.[16]

---

[7] This duty to report the accident to a police officer is not avoided by the fact that a police officer has observed the accident, if the driver has not in fact given his details to anyone. See *R. v Hay* [2006] R.T.R. 3.

[8] *Harding v Price* [1948] 1 All E.R. 283.

[9] *McDermott v DPP* [1997] R.T.R. 474: driving on for 80 yards before stopping and returning to the scene was not sufficient.

[10] What is a reasonable time will depend on the circumstances.

[11] This is a personal duty and cannot be delegated to another person.

[12] *Lee v Knapp* [1966] 3 All E.R. 961.

[13] *Ward v Rawson* [1978] R.T.R. 498.

[14] *Norling v Woolacott* [1964] S.A.S.R. 377. In this case the accident was to an unattended vehicle in a place where there were no other people or houses nearby.

[15] *Mutton v Bates (No.1)* [1984] R.T.R. 256.

[16] *Chief Constable of West Midlands Police v Billingham* [1979] R.T.R. 446.

Offence	Mode of trial	Section	Imprisonment	Fine	Disqualification	Penalty Points	Endorsement code	Sentencing Guidelines
Failing to stop after accident and give particulars or report accident	Summarily	s.170(4)	6 months	Level 5	Discretionary	5–10	AC10–not stopping AC20–not giving particulars or reporting	Fine Band B/C
Failure by driver in case of accident involving injury to another to produce evidence of insurance or security	Summarily	s.170(7)	No	Level 3	No	6	—	—

Road Traffic Act 1988, s.170(4)	**Fail to stop / report road accident**

Triable only summarily:
Maximum penalty: Level 5 fine and/or 6 months

Must endorse and may disqualify. If no disqualification, impose 5-10 points

OFFENCE SERIOUSNESS (CULPABILITY AND HARM)
A. IDENTIFY THE APPROPRIATE STARTING POINT
Starting points based on first time offender pleading not guilty

Examples of nature of activity	Starting point	Range
Minor damage/injury or stopped at scene but failed to exchange particulars or report	Band B fine	Band B fine 5 – 6 points
Moderate damage/injury or failed to stop and failed to report	Band C fine	Band C fine 7 – 8 points Consider disqualification
Serious damage/injury and/or evidence of bad driving	High level community order	Band C fine to 26 weeks custody Disqualify 6 – 12 months OR 9 – 10 points

OFFENCE SERIOUSNESS (CULPABILITY AND HARM)
B. CONSIDER THE EFFECT OF AGGRAVATING AND MITIGATING FACTORS
(OTHER THAN THOSE WITHIN EXAMPLES ABOVE)
Common aggravating and mitigating factors are identified in the pullout card. The following may be particularly relevant but these lists are not exhaustive:

Factors indicating higher culpability	Factors indicating lower culpability
1. Evidence of drink or drugs / evasion of test 2. Knowledge / suspicion that personal injury caused (where not an element of the offence) 3. Leaving injured party at scene 4. Giving false details	1. Believed identity known 2. Genuine fear of retribution 3. Subsequently reported

FORM A PRELIMINARY VIEW OF THE APPROPRIATE SENTENCE, THEN CONSIDER OFFENDER MITIGATION
Common factors are identified in the pullout card

CONSIDER A REDUCTION FOR GUILTY PLEA

CONSIDER ANCILLARY ORDERS, INCLUDING COMPENSATION
Refer to pages 142-148 for guidance on available ancillary orders

DECIDE SENTENCE

GIVE REASONS

Alternative verdicts

(Reference: Wilkinson's Road Traffic Offences, Ch.2.)

The statutory provisions governing alternative verdicts contained in the Road Traffic Offenders Act 1988 s.24 have been amended by the Road Safety Act 1996 as follows:

24 ALTERNATIVE VERDICTS: GENERAL

(A1) Where—

    (a) a person charged with manslaughter in connection with the driving of a mechanically propelled vehicle by him is found not guilty of that offence, but

    (b) the allegations in the indictment amount to or include an allegation of any of the relevant offences,

he may be convicted of that offence.

(A2) For the purposes of subsection (A1) above the following are the relevant offences—

    (a) an offence under section 1 of the Road Traffic Act 1988 (causing death by dangerous driving),

    (b) an offence under section 2 of that Act (dangerous driving),

    (c) an offence under section 3A of that Act (causing death by careless driving when under influence of drink or drugs), and

    (d) an offence under section 35 of the Offences against the Person Act 1861 (furious driving).]

(1) Where—

    (a) a person charged with an offence under a provision of the Road Traffic Act 1988 specified in the first column of the Table below (where the general nature of the offences is also indicated) is found not guilty of that offence, but

    (b) the allegations in the indictment or information (or in Scotland complaint) amount to or include an allegation of an offence under one or more of the provisions specified in the corresponding entry in the second column,

he may be convicted of that offence or of one or more of those offences.

Offence charged	Alternative
Section 1 (causing death by dangerous driving)	Section 2 (dangerous driving)

	[Section 2B (causing death by careless, or inconsiderate driving)]*
	Section 3 (careless, and inconsiderate, driving)
Section 2 (dangerous driving)	Section 3 (careless, and inconsiderate, driving)
[Section 2B (causing death by careless, or inconsiderate, driving)]*	Section 3 (careless, and inconsiderate, driving)]
Section 3A (causing death by careless driving when under influence of drink or drugs)	[Section 2B (causing death by careless, or inconsiderate, driving)]* Section 3 (careless, and inconsiderate, driving) Section 4(1) (driving when unfit to drive through drink or drugs) Section 5(1)(a) (driving with excess alcohol in breath, blood or urine) Section 7(6) (failing to provide specimen) Section 7A(6) (failing to give permission for laboratory test)
Section 4(1) (driving or attempting to drive when unfit to drive through drink or drugs) Section 5(1)(a) (driving or attempting to drive with excess alcohol in breath, blood or urine) Section 28 (dangerous cycling)	Section 4(2) (being in charge of a vehicle when unfit to drive through drink or drugs) Section 5(1)(b) (being in charge of a vehicle with excess alcohol in breath, blood or urine) Section 29 (careless, and inconsiderate, cycling)

*Note that these offences are not in force at the time of writing (April 2008).

(2) Where the offence with which a person is charged is an offence under section 3A of the Road Traffic Act 1988, subsection (1) above shall not authorise his conviction of any offence of attempting to drive.

(3) Where a person is charged with having committed an offence under section 4(1) or 5(1)(a) of the Road Traffic Act 1988 by driving a vehicle, he may be convicted of having committed an offence under the provision in question by attempting to drive.

(4) Where by virtue of this section a person is convicted before the Crown Court of an offence triable only summarily, the court shall have the same powers and duties as a magistrates' court would have had on convicting him of that offence.

(5) ...

(6) This section has effect without prejudice to section 6(3) of the Criminal Law Act 1967 ...

Alternative verdicts are not generally available in the magistrates' court, only where specifically provided for by statute. It is therefore not possible for the prosecution to seek an alternative verdict other than as provided for by s.24 of the Act; in all other cases, the prosecution must ensure that all the offences to be considered are properly laid before the court.

As a matter of good practice, the prosecutor should remind the magistrates where an alternative verdict is available, or give a clear indication when there are offences before the court which are to be considered in the alternative. The magistrates should ensure that the parties have had an opportunity to address the court before reaching a decision where an alternative verdict is available for consideration.

Section 24 does not affect the general provisions relating to alternative verdicts on trial on indictment as provided by s.6(3) of the Criminal Law Act 1967. However, conviction of an offence triable only summarily restricts the sentencing powers of the judge to those of the magistrates' court.

Causing, permitting, using

(Reference: Wilkinson's Road Traffic Offences, Ch.1.)

Offences of **causing or permitting** some sort of unlawful "use" will require the prosecution to prove an element of *mens rea* in knowledge of the facts that make the use unlawful. In the case of a limited company, that knowledge must be of someone exercising a directing mind over the company's affairs.[1] In such circumstances, to "cause" requires some degree of control or direction and implies an express or positive mandate, or some authority, from the person said to be causing the unlawful use.

Where the offence is only to "cause or permit" a contravention, not involving an unlawful use, the offence may not require proof of *mens rea* and may be one of strict liability. A positive act will still need to be proved; mere passive looking-on is insufficient.[2]

"Permission" may be express or implied, and means allowing someone other than the person giving permission to do something. If the other person is given control of the vehicle, permission may be inferred if the vehicle is left at the other person's disposal in circumstances as to carry with it a reasonable implication of a discretion or liberty to use the vehicle in the manner in which it was in fact used.[3] Anyone who has control of a vehicle on the owner's behalf can permit its use. As in the case of causing, some sort of knowledge on the part of the person giving permission will be required, although shutting one's eyes to the obvious or allowing someone to do something likely to lead to a contravention and not caring whether or not that occurs will suffice. A distinction needs to be made between knowledge of the use of the vehicle and knowledge of the unlawfulness of that use. Depending on the statutory provision, knowledge only of use of the vehicle may be sufficient, e.g. in the case of permitting a vehicle to be used without insurance, where the prosecution need not establish that the person permitting use of the vehicle knew that the user was uninsured.[4] However, where permission to use is given subject to an express condition that the user is insured, or holds a valid driving licence, the person giving permission is not liable if the user turns out not to be insured or licensed.[5] There must be an express condition attached to the permission to avoid liability, an honest albeit mistaken belief as to the facts is not sufficient.[6] The conditional permission must be given directly to the intended driver; a conditional permission given to a permitted user will not suffice if someone else then drives the vehicle, even if the

---

[1] *James and Son Ltd v Smee* [1954] 3 All E.R. 273; *Ross Hillman Ltd v Bond* [1974] R.T.R. 279.
[2] *Price v Cromack* [1975] 2 All E.R. 113.
[3] *McLeod v Buchanan* [1940] 2 All E.R. 179 at 187.
[4] *Davies v Warne* [1973] R.T.R. 217, where a conviction was upheld where both user and permitter genuinely and reasonably believed the use of the vehicle was covered by insurance.
[5] *Newbury v Davis* [1974] R.T.R. 367.
[6] *Baugh v Crago* [1975] R.T.R. 453.

conditional permission is given knowing that it is intended someone else will be driving.[7]

Offences involving **"using"** a motor vehicle normally imply strict liability, in the absence of a specific statutory defence. For example, using without insurance,[8] without most licences, or contrary to construction and use regulations. Lack of knowledge of the facts amounting to the offence, or lack of negligence is immaterial. A person driving a vehicle will normally be using it. A person with custody and control of a vehicle may be using it, even if not the driver. An owner of a vehicle is deemed to have been using it in the absence of contrary evidence.[9]

A person does not use a vehicle without insurance unless there is an element of controlling, managing or operating the vehicle as a vehicle,[10] nor does a passenger who does not procure the making of the journey.[11] A passenger who has procured the journey,[12] or is acting in joint enterprise with the driver will be liable as a user.[13]

Where the statute creates the offence of causing or permitting as well as using, only the driver, a person in the vehicle controlling the driver, a person engaged in joint enterprise with the driver, and the driver's employer while it is being used on employer's business will use it. It will be a matter of fact whether the actions of an employee have deviated from his duty and instructions sufficiently to say that the use of the vehicle is no longer on employer's business. Where the only offence is using, it may be possible to charge an owner with using if he caused the vehicle to be used by another on his behalf.

A vehicle is in use if it is stationary on a road for loading and unloading.[14] It is in use, and must be insured even where it has been left immobile, with an engine that does not work and without petrol and a battery, provided it can be moved, e.g. by pushing or releasing the brake.[15]

---

[7] *DPP v Fisher* [1992] R.T.R 93.

[8] Note the special statutory defence under s.143(3) of the Road Traffic Act 1988 for persons using a vehicle in the course of their employment.

[9] *Watson v Paterson*, noted at 121 J.P. 336, and *Ende v Cassidy* (1964) 108 S.J. 522.

[10] *Nichol v Leach* [1972] R.T.R. 416.

[11] *D v Parsons* [1960] 2 All E.R. 493.

[12] *Cobb v Williams* [1973] R.T.R. 113.

[13] *Leathley v Tatton* [1980] R.T.R. 21.

[14] *Andrews v Kershaw* [1951] 2 All E.R. 764.

[15] *Elliott v Grey* [1959] 3 All E.R. 733.

Careless, and inconsiderate, driving

(Reference: Wilkinson's Road Traffic Offences, Ch.5.)

The Road Traffic Act 1988 s.3 creates two offences, careless driving and inconsiderate driving.

3 CARELESS, AND INCONSIDERATE, DRIVING

If a person drives a mechanically propelled vehicle on a road or other public place without due care and attention, or without reasonable consideration for other persons using the road or place, he is guilty of an offence.

The Road Safety Act 2006 has amended the Road Traffic Act 1988 by inserting at 3ZA a statutory definition of careless, or inconsiderate driving, as follows:

3ZA MEANING OF CARELESS, OR INCONSIDERATE, DRIVING

(1) This section has effect for the purposes of sections 2B and 3 above and section 3A below.

(2) A person is to be regarded as driving without due care and attention if (and only if) the way he drives falls below what would be expected of a competent and careful driver.

(3) In determining for the purposes of subsection (2) above what would be expected of a careful and competent driver in a particular case, regard shall be had not only to the circumstances of which he could be expected to be aware but also to any circumstances shown to have been within the knowledge of the accused.

(4) A person is to be regarded as driving without reasonable consideration for other persons only if those persons are inconvenienced by his driving.

The statutory definition has simply enacted the familiar test laid down through case law and is similar to that for the tort of negligence, i.e. whether the driving has departed from the standard of a reasonable, competent and prudent driver (shortened to "competent and careful") taking into account all the circumstances of the particular case[1] (now clarified to cover circumstances of which a driver is expected to be aware, and circumstances of which he was in

---

[1] *Scott v Warren* [1974] R.T.R. 104.

fact aware). It is submitted that the old case-law remains relevant in interpreting the new statutory definition.

Whether driving is **careless** will be a matter of fact to be determined. Each situation will be unique; actions that amount to careless driving in one situation may not be in another. It is irrelevant whether the driving is deliberate or an error of judgment, or due to inexperience. However, if a driver is suddenly confronted with an emergency situation, the driving must be judged by whether it was reasonable to react as the driver did in such circumstances. The Highway Code is a good guide to the required standard of driving, but not conclusive.

It is a defence that a vehicle had a sudden defect of which the defendant neither knew nor should have been expected to know.[2] The defence of automatism may also be raised. However, a defendant who is aware of a defect, or aware of an illness or of being over-tired such that his ability to drive is likely to be affected, will be guilty of careless driving if his driving is so affected.

The prosecution may not need to prove exactly what happened, and evidence of the result of the driving may be sufficient. The facts must be such that in the absence of any explanation such as mechanical defect, illness or some other explanation, they give rise to an inevitable inference that the defendant was driving carelessly. In such a situation, it is said that the facts speak for themselves, and it can be safely concluded that the driving must have departed from the required standard.[3] This will often be the case where, for example, a vehicle has left the road and collided with a wall or pole, or ended up in a ditch, for no apparent reason. However, once an explanation is put forward, unless it is clearly fanciful, the prosecution will be required to prove it untrue beyond reasonable doubt.[4] The court should not speculate as to what may have happened in the absence of evidence to support it.

Driving will be **inconsiderate** if other road users were, in fact, inconvenienced. Inconsiderate driving will always amount to careless driving, since the standard will inevitably have been departed from; the careful and competent driver does not drive inconsiderately.

(See also **Driving, Mechanically propelled vehicle and Road**.)

---

[2] *R. v Spurge* [1961] 2 All E.R. 688.
[3] *Bensley v Smith* [1972] Crim. L.R. 239.
[4] *Butty v Davey* [1972] Crim. L.R. 48.

Careless and inconsiderate driving

Offence	Mode of trial	Section	Imprisonment	Fine	Disqualification	Penalty Points	Endorsement Code	Sentencing Guidelines
Careless or inconsiderate driving	Summary	s.3	—	Level 5	Discretionary	3–9	CD10 careless driving; CD20 inconsiderate driving; CD30 in Scotland (both offences)	Fine level A/B/C

Careless driving (drive without due care and attention)	Road Traffic Act 1988, s.3

Triable only summarily:
Maximum penalty: Level 5 fine

Must endorse and may disqualify. If no disqualification, impose 3-9 points

OFFENCE SERIOUSNESS (CULPABILITY AND HARM) A. IDENTIFY THE APPROPRIATE STARTING POINT Starting points based on first time offender pleading not guilty		
Examples of nature of activity	Starting point	Range
Momentary lapse of concentration or misjudgement at low speed	Band A fine	Band A fine 3 – 4 points
Loss of control due to speed, mishandling or insufficient attention to road conditions, or carelessly turning right across on-coming traffic	Band B fine	Band B fine 5 – 6 points
Overtaking manoeuvre at speed resulting in collision of vehicles, or driving bordering on the dangerous	Band C fine	Band C fine Consider disqualification OR 7 – 9 points

OFFENCE SERIOUSNESS (CULPABILITY AND HARM) B. CONSIDER THE EFFECT OF AGGRAVATING AND MITIGATING FACTORS (OTHER THAN THOSE WITHIN EXAMPLES ABOVE) Common aggravating and mitigating factors are identified in the pullout card. The following may be particularly relevant but these lists are not exhaustive:	
Factors indicating higher culpability 1. Excessive speed 2. Carrying out other tasks while driving 3. Carrying passengers or heavy load 4. Tiredness Factors indicating greater degree of harm 1. Injury to others 2. Damage to other vehicles or property 3. High level of traffic or pedestrians in vicinity 4. Location e.g. near school when children are likely to be present	Factors indicating lower culpability 1. Minor risk 2. Inexperience of driver 3. Sudden change in road or weather conditions

FORM A PRELIMINARY VIEW OF THE APPROPRIATE SENTENCE, THEN CONSIDER OFFENDER MITIGATION
Common factors are identified in the pullout card

CONSIDER A REDUCTION FOR GUILTY PLEA

CONSIDER ORDERING DISQUALIFICATION UNTIL APPROPRIATE DRIVING TEST PASSED

CONSIDER ANCILLARY ORDERS, INCLUDING COMPENSATION
Refer to pages 142-148 for guidance on available ancillary orders

DECIDE SENTENCE

GIVE REASONS

Careless, and inconsiderate, driving when under the influence of drink/drugs, Causing death by

(Reference: Wilkinson's Road Traffic Offences, Ch.5.)

The Road Traffic Act 1988 s.3A creates the following offences:

3A CAUSING DEATH BY CARELESS DRIVING WHEN UNDER INFLUENCE OF DRINK OR DRUGS

(1) If a person causes the death of another person by driving a mechanically propelled vehicle on a road or other public place without due care and attention, or without reasonable consideration[1] for other persons using the road or place, and—

(a) he is, at the time when he is driving, unfit to drive through drink or drugs, or

(b) he has consumed so much alcohol that the proportion of it in his breath, blood or urine at that time exceeds the prescribed limit, or

(c) he is, within 18 hours after that time, required to provide a specimen in pursuance of section 7 of this Act, but without reasonable excuse fails to provide it,

he is guilty of an offence.[2]

(2) For the purposes of this section a person shall be taken to be unfit to drive at any time when his ability to drive properly is impaired.

(3) Subsection (1)(b) and (c) above shall not apply in relation to a person driving a mechanically propelled vehicle other than a motor vehicle.

These offences are triable only on indictment and must be sent to the Crown Court for trial under s.51 of the Crime and Disorder Act 1998. The magistrates' court will give preliminary directions for the management of the case and fix a next hearing date at the Crown Court. (See **Procedure.**)

---

[1] Note that the statutory definition inserted in s.3ZA of the Road Traffic Act 1988 is now in force and applies to offences under s.3A (see **Careless, and inconsiderate, driving**).

[2] Note that the Road Safety Act 2006 s.31 (now in force) has amended this section to cover the situation where a specimen has been taken and permission for analysis is required under s.7A of the Road Traffic Act 1988. It is an offence to refuse to give permission for the laboratory analysis and conviction of that offence under s.7(A)(6) is available as an alternative verdict (see **Alternative verdicts**).

Offence	Mode of trial	Section	Imprisonment	Fine	Disqualification	Penalty points	Endorsement code
Causing death by careless driving when under influence of drink or drugs, etc.	Only on indictment	s.3A	14 years	Unlimited	Obligatory (minimum 2 years)	3–11	CD40 (unfit; drink) CD50 (unfit; drugs) CD60 (excess alcohol) CD70 (fail provide specimen)

*Careless, or inconsiderate, driving, Causing death by

*These are new offences created by the Road Safety Act 2006, not yet in force. A new s.2B will be inserted into the Road Traffic Act 1988.

2B   CAUSING DEATH BY CARELESS, OR INCONSIDERATE, DRIVING

A person who causes the death of another person by driving a mechanically propelled vehicle on a road or other public place without due care and attention, or without reasonable consideration for other persons using the road or place, is guilty of an offence.

The new statutory definitions of the meaning of careless, or inconsiderate, driving in s.3ZA of the Road Traffic Act 1988 will apply (see **Careless, and inconsiderate, driving**).

The new offences will be triable either way, and so may, if appropriate, be tried in a magistrates' court. Section 24(1) of the Road Traffic Offenders Act 1988 will be amended to allow a court to reach an alternative verdict of careless and inconsiderate driving. (See **Procedure** and **Alternative verdicts**.)

The same penalty will apply to both offences; if tried summarily, a maximum of 12 months imprisonment (note that currently a magistrates court may only impose up to six months imprisonment per offence) or a fine up to £5,000, or both. On indictment, the maximum penalty is five years imprisonment and or a fine. Disqualification is obligatory, but where disqualification is not imposed, endorsement is obligatory with variable penalty points from 3–11.

*Causing death by driving unlicensed, disqualified, or uninsured

*These are new offences created by the Road Safety Act 2006, not yet in force. A new section will be inserted into the Road Traffic Act 1988.

3ZB Causing Death by Driving: Unlicensed, Disqualified or Uninsured Drivers

A person is guilty of an offence under this section if he causes the death of another person by driving a motor vehicle on a road and, at the time when he is driving, the circumstances are such that he is committing an offence under—

    (a) section 87(1) of this Act (driving otherwise than in accordance with a licence),

    (b) section 103(1)(b) of this Act (driving while disqualified), or

    (c) section 143 of this Act (using motor vehicle while uninsured or unsecured against third party risks).

These new offences will be triable either way, and so may, if appropriate, be tried in a magistrates' court. An alternative verdict of careless and inconsiderate driving will not be available for these offences. (See **Procedure** and **Alternative verdicts**.)

The same penalty will apply for each of the offences; if tried summarily, a maximum of 12 months imprisonment (note that currently a magistrates court may only impose up to six months imprisonment for individual offences) or a fine up to £5,000, or both. On indictment, the maximum penalty will be two years imprisonment and/or a fine. Disqualification will be obligatory, but where disqualification is not imposed, endorsement will be obligatory with variable penalty points from 3–11.

Dangerous driving

(Reference: Wilkinson's Road Traffic Offences, Ch.5.)

The Road Traffic Act 1988 s.2 creates the offence of dangerous driving.

2   DANGEROUS DRIVING

A person who drives a mechanically propelled vehicle dangerously on a road or other public place is guilty of an offence.

2A   MEANING OF DANGEROUS DRIVING

(1) For the purposes of sections 1 and 2 above a person is to be regarded as driving dangerously if (and, subject to subsection (2) below, only if)—

   (a) the way he drives falls far below what would be expected of a competent and careful driver, and
   (b) it would be obvious to a competent and careful driver that driving in that way would be dangerous.

(2) A person is also to be regarded as driving dangerously for the purposes of sections 1 and 2 above if it would be obvious to a competent and careful driver that driving the vehicle in its current state would be dangerous.

(3) In subsections (1) and (2) above "dangerous" refers to danger either of injury to any person or of serious damage to property; and in determining for the purposes of those subsections what would be expected of, or obvious to, a competent and careful driver in a particular case, regard shall be had not only to the circumstances of which he could be expected to be aware but also to any circumstances shown to have been within the knowledge of the accused.

(4) In determining for the purposes of subsection (2) above the state of a vehicle, regard may be had to anything attached to or carried on or in it and to the manner in which it is attached or carried.

The offence of dangerous driving is triable either way, and so may, if appropriate, be tried in a magistrates' court. An alternative verdict of careless and inconsiderate driving is available for this offence. (See **Procedure** and **Alternative verdicts**.)

The *actus reus* required is driving in a manner which falls far below what would be expected of a careful and competent driver in circumstances in which it would be obvious to such a competent and careful driver that driving in that way, or driving the vehicle in its current state, would be dangerous. The offence may be committed where it is the driver who is in the dangerously defective state, whether through drink[1] or diabetes.[2] There is a very clear qualitative distinction between the standard of driving required for an offence of dangerous driving from that of the lesser offence of careless driving. (See **Careless, and inconsiderate driving**.)

The offence may be committed not only on a road but in any public place, and covers any mechanically propelled vehicle; it is not limited to motor vehicles.

The "danger" is of personal injury or serious damage to property. It is not necessary to show any actual injury or serious damage to property, only the obvious risk of such.

It is not necessary to show that the defendant was conscious of the consequences of his actions, only that he was conscious of what he was doing. The test of apprehending danger is an objective one to be judged by reference to what would be obvious to a competent and careful driver. However, s.2A(3) requires that in determining what would be expected of or obvious to such a driver, the circumstances of the particular case must be considered together with any actual knowledge of the defendant.[3] However, what the defendant believes to be the case, whether genuine or not, is not a relevant factor.[4] A mistaken action, such as pressing the accelerator rather than the brake, is no defence to dangerous driving.[5]

The defence of necessity can only be raised where the defendant can establish that the situation was such that it was necessary to have driven dangerously, and there was no other reasonable way of dealing with the emergency without driving in that manner.[6]

---

[1] *R. v Woodward (Terence)* [1995] R.T.R. 130.

[2] *R. v Marison* [1996] Crim. L.R. 909.

[3] Circumstances such as his other special driving skills or his complete lack of experience can be taken into account in applying the objective test: *Milton v CPS* [2007] EWHC 532 (Admin).

[4] *R. v Collins (Lezlie)* [1997] R.T.R. 439.

[5] *Att-Gen's Reference (No.4 of 2000)* [2001] EWCA Crim 780; [2001] R.T.R. 27.

[6] *R v May Arnaot* [2008] EWCA Crim 121 provides a useful short summary of the nature of such a defence and when it might apply.

Offence	Mode of trial	Section	Imprisonment	Fine	Disqualification	Penalty points	Endorsement code	Sentencing guidelines
Dangerous driving	a) on indictment	s.2	2 years	Unlimited	Obligatory compulsory retest	3–11	DD40	—
	b) summarily	s.2	6 months	Level 5	Obligatory compulsory retest	3–11	DD40	Consider community order/ custody: disq 12 months (at least) and order retest

Dangerous driving	Road Traffic Act 1988, s.2

Triable either way:
Maximum when tried summarily: Level 5 fine and/or 6 months   Maximum when tried on indictment: 2 years

- Must endorse and disqualify for at least 12 months. Must order extended re-test
- Must disqualify for **at least** 2 years if offender has had two or more disqualifications for periods of 56 days or more in preceding 3 years – **refer to page 159 and consult your legal adviser for further guidance**

If there is a delay in sentencing after conviction, consider interim disqualification

OFFENCE SERIOUSNESS (CULPABILITY AND HARM)
A. IDENTIFY THE APPROPRIATE STARTING POINT
Starting points based on first time offender pleading not guilty

Examples of nature of activity	Starting point	Range
Single incident where little or no damage or risk of personal injury	Medium level community order	Low level community order to high level community order Disqualify 12 – 15 months
Incident(s) involving excessive speed or showing off, especially on busy roads or in built-up area; OR Single incident where little or no damage or risk of personal injury but offender was disqualified driver	12 weeks custody	High level community order to 26 weeks custody Disqualify 15 – 24 months.
Prolonged bad driving involving deliberate disregard for safety of others; OR Incident(s) involving excessive speed or showing off, especially on busy roads or in built-up area, by disqualified driver; OR Driving as described in box above while being pursued by police	Crown Court	Crown Court

OFFENCE SERIOUSNESS (CULPABILITY AND HARM)
B. CONSIDER THE EFFECT OF AGGRAVATING AND MITIGATING FACTORS
(OTHER THAN THOSE WITHIN EXAMPLES ABOVE)
Common aggravating and mitigating factors are identified in the pullout card. The following may be particularly relevant but these lists are not exhaustive:

Factors indicating higher culpability	Factors indicating lower culpability
1. Disregarding warnings of others 2. Evidence of alcohol or drugs 3. Carrying out other tasks while driving 4. Carrying passengers or heavy load 5. Tiredness 6. Aggressive driving, such as driving much too close to vehicle in front, racing, inappropriate attempts to overtake, or cutting in after overtaking 7. Driving when knowingly suffering from a medical condition which significantly impairs the offender's driving skills 8. Driving a poorly maintained or dangerously loaded vehicle, especially where motivated by commercial concerns Factors indicating greater degree of harm 1. Injury to others 2. Damage to other vehicles or property	1. Genuine emergency 2. Speed not excessive 3. Offence due to inexperience rather than irresponsibility of driver

FORM A PRELIMINARY VIEW OF THE APPROPRIATE SENTENCE, THEN CONSIDER OFFENDER MITIGATION
Common factors are identified in the pullout card

CONSIDER A REDUCTION FOR GUILTY PLEA

CONSIDER ANCILLARY ORDERS, INCLUDING COMPENSATION AND DEPRIVATION OF PROPERTY
Refer to pages 142-148 for guidance on available ancillary orders

DECIDE SENTENCE
GIVE REASONS

© The Sentencing Guidelines Council

Dangerous driving, Causing death by

(Reference: Wilkinson's Road Traffic Offences, Ch.5.)

The Road Traffic Act 1988 s.1 creates the offence of causing death by dangerous driving.

1   CAUSING DEATH BY DANGEROUS DRIVING

A person who causes the death of another person by driving a mechanically propelled vehicle dangerously on a road or other public place is guilty of an offence.

This offence is triable only on indictment and must be sent to the Crown Court for trial under s.51 of the Crime and Disorder Act 1998. The magistrates' court will give preliminary directions for the management of the case and fix a next hearing date at the Crown Court. (See **Procedure**.)

Offence	Mode of trial	Section	Imprisonment	Fine	Disqualification	Penalty points	Endorsement code	Sentencing guidelines
Causing death by dangerous driving	Only on indictment	s.1	14 years	Unlimited	Obligatory (minimum 2 years) compulsory retest	3–11	DD80	—

Disclosure

(Reference: Wilkinson's Road Traffic Offences, Ch.2.)

There is no general duty of disclosure in a magistrates' court. The Criminal Procedure and Investigations Act 1996 and the Criminal Procedure Rules 2005 (CPR 2005) impose duties on the prosecution to disclose material at various stages of the proceedings. The defence may be required to disclose information in certain circumstances (e.g. when relying on an alibi defence, or in a defence statement).

Information the prosecutor is, or may be, required to provide:

Advance information

Provision of advance information is a duty on the prosecution that arises on request by the defendant before a plea has been entered and applies only to offences triable either way. It does not apply in respect of offences which are summary only or triable only on indictment.[1] This information is to enable the defendant to decide on plea and venue. The court must be satisfied that the defendant is aware of his right to receive advance information.[2]

The information that may be requested, and the procedure to be followed is contained in CPR 2005 r.21. There is no entitlement to be provided with all the actual prosecution evidence at this stage in the proceedings. There is no entitlement to disclosure of any unused material at this stage in the proceedings.[3]

The prosecutor may comply with a request for advance information either:

a) by providing a copy of those parts of every written statement which contain information as to the facts and matters[4] of which the prosecutor proposes to adduce evidence in the proceedings; or

b) a summary of those facts and matters.[5]

Where reference is made to a document on which the prosecutor proposes to rely, either a copy of that document or such information as is necessary to enable

---

[1] The restriction of entitlement to advance information to offences triable either way applies to youths as well as adults, even though youths must be "tried summarily" unless s.24 of the Magistrates' Courts Act 1980 provides otherwise. However, prosecutors may be prepared to provide case summaries in appropriate cases, even where the offence is not triable either way, to assist defence advocates and since the introduction of CJSSS schemes around the country, a bundle of case papers is usually provided at, or before, first hearings.

[2] CPR 2005 r.21.5.

[3] Subject to any remaining common law provisions. See *R. v DPP Ex p. Lee* (1999) 2 Cr.App.R. 304.

[4] Rule 21.4(1) permits the prosecutor to decline to disclose a particular fact or matter if disclosure might lead to intimidation or attempted intimidation of a prosecution witness or interference with the course of justice.

[5] The Rules do not specify that such a summary has to be written or otherwise recorded.

a request to be made to inspect the document must be provided (r.21.3(3)). The law is still unclear as to what is to be regarded as a "document" under the rule.[6]

Rule 21.6(1) states that if a request for advance information has been made and the requirements of the rules not complied with, the court shall adjourn proceedings for the purposes of provision of advance information unless it is satisfied that the conduct of the case for the accused will not be substantially prejudiced by non-compliance with the requirement.[7]

The only power the court has is to adjourn proceedings pending compliance by the prosecution with the requirement to provide advance information. The court does not have the power to order the prosecution to provide specific material by way of advance information.[8]

Provision of prosecution evidence

The provision of prosecution evidence in summary trials is a duty on the prosecution that arises only after a not-guilty plea has been entered. It is not regulated by any statutory provisions, but is covered by the Attorney General's Guidelines on Disclosure (April 2005) (AG Guidelines). Paragraph 57 requires the prosecution to provide the defendant with all the evidence upon which they intend to rely at trial (in so far as it has not already been provided as advance information, where that duty arises) to allow the defendant and his legal adviser sufficient time properly to consider the evidence before it is called. Standard directions[9] currently set a time limit of 28 days from plea for prosecution to provide such evidence.

Disclosure of unused prosecution material

This is a duty on the prosecution that arises only after a not-guilty plea has been entered.[10] Disclosure of unused material is governed by the Criminal

---

[6] In *R. v Calderdale Magistrates' Court Ex p. Donahue and Cutler* [2001] Crim. L.R. 141 the court granted an adjournment to allow the defendant to view a video constituting the identification evidence and referred to in the advance information. The case was founded on a concession that the video was a "document" under the Rules, a point which remains to be formally decided. In *R. (on the application of the DPP) v Croydon Magistrates' Court* [2001] EWHC Admin 552 reference in a case summary to results of DNA samples did not amount to reference to a document and the prosecution was not obliged to provide further documentary information about the DNA profiling at that stage of the proceedings.

[7] Rule 21.6(2) provides that where the court decides not to adjourn, a record of that decision and the reasons why the court was satisfied that the conduct of the case for the accused would not be substantially prejudiced by non-compliance with the requirement must be entered in the court register.

[8] *R. v Dunmow Justices Ex p. Nash* (1993) 157 J.P. 1153, per Watkins L.J. "the only power under the rules given to the Justices, where they are satisfied that a defendant has not had proper disclosure from the prosecution, is to adjourn the matter before the Court". This decision needs to be considered in the light of the case management powers contained in the Criminal Procedure Rules 2005.

[9] "Standard directions" refers to the default directions set out in the case progression forms for use in magistrates' courts in accordance with the Consolidated Criminal Practice Direction.

[10] Duties also arise in relation to cases being sent or committed for trial to the Crown Court.

Procedure and Investigations Act 1996 (CPIA).[11] The law is set out in the Act as amended by Pt V of the Criminal Justice Act 2003. The April 2005 edition of the Code of Practice under s.23(1) of the Act applies.[12]

The revised test for disclosure of unused material requires the prosecutor to disclose any prosecution material which might reasonably be considered capable of undermining the case for the prosecution against the accused or of assisting the case for the accused. This one test applies throughout. Standard directions allow 28 days following plea for initial disclosure to be provided.

The defence statement

Provision of a defence statement is voluntary in relation to trial in the magistrate's court (s.6 of the CPIA). However, a defence statement is a necessary pre-requisite for an application for specific disclosure under s.8 of the CPIA, and the court cannot make any orders for disclosure of unused prosecution material under the Act if no such statement has been served. Service of the defence statement is therefore a critical stage in the disclosure process, and a defendant will want to give consideration at an early stage as to whether to serve such a statement.

Defence statements must comply with the requirements set out in the Act. Enhanced requirements apply to defence statements under s.6A, as amended by the Criminal Justice Act 2003. The defence statement must spell out, in detail, the nature of the defence, and particular defences relied upon; it must identify the matters of fact upon which the defendant takes issue with the prosecution, and the reason why, in relation to each disputed matter of fact. It must further identify any point of law (including points as to the admissibility of evidence, or abuse of process) which the defendant proposes to take, and identify authorities relied on in relation to each point of law.[13] Where an alibi defence is relied upon, the particulars given must comply with s.6A(2)(a) and (b) of the Act.

Standard directions require that a defence statement, if there is to be one, must be served within 14 days of the date upon which the prosecution has complied with, or purported to comply with the duty to provide initial disclosure.[14] Where it is not possible to serve a properly drafted defence statement within the 14 day period, application may be made for an extension of time under reg.3(1) of the CPIA 1996 (Defence Disclosure Time Limits) Regulations 1997. Such applications must be made in writing in accordance with CPR 2005 r.25.7, and must be made before the time limit expires (reg.3(2)).[15]

---

[11] There may be occasions when the prosecutor, pursuant to surviving common law rules of disclosure, ought to disclose an item or items of unused material in advance of disclosure under the Act, e.g. to assist a defendant in making a bail application. However, once the Act applies, the common law no longer applies. See *R. v DPP Ex p. Lee* (1999) 2 Cr.App.R. 304. The circumstances in which common law disclosure should be given are rare and the surviving common law rules cannot be cited to obtain disclosure in advance of the statutory duty arising, or wider disclosure than would be available under the Act.

[12] See SI 2005/985.

[13] See s.6A(1) of the CPIA.

[14] See also reg.2 of the CPIA 1996 (Defence Disclosure Time Limits) Regulations 1997.

[15] Applications must specify why it is not possible to provide a defence statement before the expiration of the time period and specify the number of days by which the accused wishes that period to be extended.

Late service of a defence statement does not, of itself, permit the prosecution to ignore it, nor does it preclude the court from considering a proper application under s.8 of the CPIA.[16]

If the defence have a reasonable basis to claim disclosure has been inadequate, they should make a formal application under s.8 of the CPIA. The procedure for making such an application is set out in CPR 2005 r.25.6. This requires written notice in the form prescribed by r.25.6(2). The prosecutor is entitled to 14 days within which to agree to provide the specific disclosure requested or to request a hearing in order to make representations in relation to the defence application (r.25.6(5)).

Third party disclosure

The disclosure of unused material that remains in the hands of a third party is an area of the law that causes difficulty.[17] The CPIA and code of practice are not directed to creating duties for third parties to follow.[18] There is no specific procedure governing the disclosure of material held by third parties in criminal proceedings. The provisions of s.97 of the Magistrates' Courts Act 1980 (issue of a witness summons or warrant) can be used in order to obtain material in the hands of a third party. However the test to be applied is not the same test as under the CPIA. The material in question must be "material" evidence, i.e. immediately admissible in evidence in the proceedings.[19]

Material held by government departments or other Crown agencies will not be prosecution material for the purposes of s.3(2) or s.8(4) of the CPIA, if it has not been inspected, recorded and retained during the course of the relevant criminal investigation. However, the Attorney General's Guidelines impose a duty on the investigators and prosecutors to consider whether such departments or bodies have material which may satisfy the test for disclosure under the Act. Where this is the case, they must seek appropriate disclosure from such bodies, who should themselves have an identified point for such enquiries.[20]

Where material is held by a third party such as a local authority, a social services department, hospital or business, investigators and prosecutors may seek to make arrangements to inspect the material with a view to applying the appropriate test for disclosure to it and determining whether any or all of the material should be retained, recorded and, in due course, disclosed to the defendant. In considering the latter, the investigators and the prosecutor will establish whether the holder of the material wishes to raise public interest immunity (PII) issues,[21] as a result of which the material may have to be placed before the court.

---

[16] See *DPP v Wood; DPP v McGillicuddy* [2005] EWHC 2986, both cases where disclosure was sought of material relating to breathalyser machines.

[17] Note the decision of the court in *DPP v Wood; DPP v McGillicuddy* [2005] EWHC 2986 to the effect that material in the hands of Intoximeters UK is not prosecution material, but third party material.

[18] See *DPP v Wood; DPP v McGillicuddy* [2005] EWHC 2986.

[19] See *R. v Reading Justices Ex p. Berkshire CC* [1996] 1 Cr.App.R. 239; *R. v Derby Magistrates' Court Ex p. B* [1996] A.C. 487; [1996] 1 Cr.App.R. 385; *R. v Alibhai and others* [2004] EWCA Crim 681.

[20] See paras 47 to 51 of the Guidelines.

[21] Section 16 of the CPIA gives such a party a right to make representations to the court.

Where a third party declines to allow inspection of the material, or requires the prosecution to obtain an order before handing over copies of the material, the prosecutor will need to consider whether it is appropriate to obtain a witness summons under s.97 of the Magistrates' Court Act 1980, if the statutory requirements are satisfied, and where the prosecutor considers that the material may satisfy the appropriate test for disclosure.[22] If the prosecutor declines to make such an application, there is nothing to prevent the defendant from so applying. However, the witness summons procedure is for obtaining relevant information to be given in evidence, not for "disclosure" of material to the defendant.

The court will decline to make an order if it considers the application in the nature of a "fishing" expedition in relation to third party material and may even consider making an order for wasted costs where an application is clearly unmeritorious and ill-conceived. Many of the recent cases on disclosure have arisen out of applications concerning technical material relating to approved devices used in the detection of road traffic offences (e.g. breathalyser machines, speed check devices, etc.); the observations made in *R. v Skegness Magistrates' Court Ex p. Cardy* [1985] R.T.R. 49 remain relevant.[23]

---

[22] *R. v Alibhai and ors* (above) makes it clear that the prosecutor has a "margin of consideration" in this regard.

[23] per Robert Goff J. (later Lord Goff) "It is important to bear in mind . . . that a witness summons must not be issued under s.97 of the Act of 1980 as a disguised attempt to obtain discovery. Nor can a witness summons be issued under s.97 summoning a person to produce documents at the hearing, when the documents are not likely to be material evidence, but it is merely desired to have them in court for the purposes of cross-examination."

Disqualification—General Principles

(Reference: Wilkinson's Road Traffic Offences, Ch.20.)

The Road Traffic Offenders Act s.37:

37 EFFECT OF ORDER OF DISQUALIFICATION

(1) Where the holder of a licence is disqualified by an order of a court, the licence shall be treated as being revoked with effect from the beginning of the period of disqualification.

(1A) Where—

    (a) the disqualification is for a fixed period shorter than 56 days in respect of an offence involving obligatory endorsement, or

    (b) the order is made under section 26 of this Act,

subsection (1) above shall not prevent the licence from again having effect at the end of the period of disqualification.

(2) Where the holder of the licence appeals against the order and the disqualification is suspended under section 39 of this Act, the period of disqualification shall be treated for the purpose of subsection (1) above as beginning on the day on which the disqualification ceases to be suspended.

(3) Notwithstanding anything in Part III of the Road Traffic Act 1988, a person disqualified by an order of a court under section 36 of this Act is (unless he is also disqualified otherwise than by virtue of such an order) entitled to obtain and to hold a provisional licence and to drive a motor vehicle in accordance with the conditions subject to which the provisional licence is granted.

An order for disqualification prohibits the driving of a motor vehicle of any type on a road which is a highway or to which the public have access during the period of disqualification. An order made by a British court has effect throughout Great Britain and Northern Ireland and will in due course apply in EC member states.[1]

Disqualification does not prevent driving on private land or on places which are not roads. An order for disqualification covers all types of motor vehicles for all purposes.

The effect of an order for disqualification is to revoke any licence issued under the 1988 Act where the period of disqualification is for 56 days or more. Shorter

---

[1] See Wilkinson's at 20.13–20.15.

periods of disqualification do not result in revocation, but the licence ceases to have effect until the end of the disqualification period. Although an order for disqualification prohibits the holding or obtaining a licence under the 1988 Act and does not affect the validity of foreign or international driving licences, a disqualified driver will still be committing an offence if he drives within the jurisdiction, notwithstanding the fact that he is the holder of a valid foreign permit.[2]

Although there is power to do so, courts may be reluctant to impose an order for disqualification in absence, even on an offender who is "deemed" present because his legal representative attends, unless satisfied that he is aware he may be disqualified and the effect of such an order. A court may not impose an order for disqualification where an offender has been convicted in his absence under the procedure for pleading guilty by post contained in s.12 of the Magistrates' Court Act 1980, unless he has been given the opportunity of attending at an adjourned hearing and warned that the court is considering making an order for disqualification.[3] When a court is considering making an order for disqualification, it should indicate as much and invite the parties to address the issue before making such an order.

Orders made may not be prospective and must commence from the moment the order is pronounced, and will run concurrently with any other order of disqualification, whether imposed at the same time or already existing. A period of disqualification must be specified, and may be expressed to be "for life". However, a lengthy period of disqualification should not be imposed unless the defendant's driving record shows that the public requires protection against his being allowed to drive. The court should impose a period of disqualification which is appropriate to the facts of the case.

Note that where the Mental Health Act 1983 s.37(3) applies, no order for disqualification can be made.

Appeals against Orders for Disqualification

The Road Traffic Offenders Act 1988 s.38 allows for an appeal to be made against an order for disqualification, as if it were a conviction.

38 APPEAL AGAINST DISQUALIFICATION

(1) A person disqualified by an order of a magistrates' court under section 34 or 35 of this Act may appeal against the order in the same manner as against a conviction.

Section 39 of the Road Traffic Offenders Act 1988 permits the disqualifying court to suspend any order for disqualification pending an appeal. The appellate court has a similar power under s.40. The statutory provisions require there to

---

[2] The Motor Vehicles (International Circulation) Order 1975 (SI 1975/1208) applies.
[3] s.11(4) of the Magistrates' Courts Act 1980.

be an appeal pending, and the requisite notice will need to have been lodged. If magistrates refuse to suspend an order where an appeal against their decision is pending, the defendant can apply to the appellate court.

39 SUSPENSION OF DISQUALIFICATION PENDING APPEAL

(1) Any court in England and Wales (whether a magistrates' court or another) which makes an order disqualifying a person may, if it thinks fit, suspend the disqualification pending an appeal against the order.

40 POWER OF APPELLATE COURTS IN ENGLAND AND WALES TO SUSPEND DISQUALIFICATION

(1) This section applies where a person has been convicted by or before a court in England and Wales of an offence involving obligatory or discretionary disqualification and has been ordered to be disqualified; and in the following provisions of this section—

  (a) any reference to a person ordered to be disqualified is to be construed as a reference to a person so convicted and so ordered to be disqualified, and

  (b) any reference to his sentence includes a reference to the order of disqualification and to any other order made on his conviction and, accordingly, any reference to an appeal against his sentence includes a reference to an appeal against any order forming part of his sentence.

(2) Where a person ordered to be disqualified—

  (a) appeals to the Crown Court, or

  (b) appeals or applies for leave to appeal to the Court of Appeal,

  against his conviction or his sentence, the Crown Court or, as the case may require, the Court of Appeal may, if it thinks fit, suspend the disqualification.

(3) . . .

(4) Where a person ordered to be disqualified makes an application in respect of the decision of the court in question under section 111 of the Magistrates' Courts Act 1980 (statement of case by magistrates' court) or section 28 of the Supreme Court Act 1981 (statement of case by Crown Court) the High Court may, if it thinks fit, suspend the disqualification.

(5) Where a person ordered to be disqualified—

  (a) applies to the High Court for an order of certiorari to remove into the High Court any proceedings of a magistrates' court or of the

Crown Court, being proceedings in or in consequence of which he was convicted or his sentence was passed, or

(b) applies to the High Court for leave to make such an application,

the High Court may, if it thinks fit, suspend the disqualification.

(6) Any power of a court under the preceding provisions of this section to suspend the disqualification of any person is a power to do so on such terms as the court thinks fit.

The decision whether or not to suspend an order for disqualification is an exercise of the court's discretion, which must be exercised judicially. The mere fact that a notice of appeal has been lodged does not entitle a defendant to have a disqualification suspended.

Where an appeal is lost or abandoned, the disqualification will immediately become effective. As driving disqualifications result in revocation of the licence (except where of less than 56 days duration), in such circumstances the licence will be automatically revoked. Any days during which disqualification ran prior to suspension will be deducted from the period running from the date of the appeal, or abandonment of appeal.

Applying for or obtaining a licence while disqualified

Before a person may drive again after serving a period of disqualification lasting 56 days or more, he must apply for a driving licence, as his previous licence will have been revoked by the disqualification. He may drive again once his application for a new licence has been received. However, if he obtains a valid licence while still disqualified, he commits an offence under s.103(1)(a) of the Road Traffic Act 1988 (see **Driving while disqualified for holding or obtaining a licence**). Applications for the grant of a licence may be dealt with up to two months before the date the licence is to take effect.

Orders for interim disqualification

The Road Traffic Offenders Act 1988 s.26 sets out the circumstances in which the court may impose an interim disqualification.

26 Interim Disqualification

(1) Where a magistrates' court—

(a) commits an offender to the Crown Court under section 6 of the Powers of Criminal Courts (Sentencing) Act 2000 or any enactment mentioned in subsection (4) of that section, or

(b) remits an offender to another magistrates' court under section 10 of that Act,

to be dealt with for an offence involving obligatory or discretionary disqualification, it may order him to be disqualified until he has been dealt with in respect of the offence.

(2) Where a court in England and Wales—

    (a) defers passing sentence on an offender under section 1 of that Act in respect of an offence involving obligatory or discretionary disqualification, or

    (b) adjourns after convicting an offender of such an offence but before dealing with him for the offence,

it may order the offender to be disqualified until he has been dealt with in respect of the offence.

(3) . . .

(4) Subject to subsection (5) below, an order under this section shall cease to have effect at the end of the period of six months beginning with the day on which it is made, if it has not ceased to have effect before that time.

(5) . . .

(6) Where a court orders a person to be disqualified under this section ("the first order"), no court shall make a further order under this section in respect of the same offence or any offence in respect of which an order could have been made under this section at the time the first order was made.

(7) Where a court makes an order under this section in respect of any person it must—

    (a) require him to produce to the court any licence held by him and its counterpart, and

    (b) retain the licence and counterpart until it deals with him or (as the case may be) cause them to be sent to the proper officer of the court which is to deal with him.

(7A) In subsection (7) above "proper officer" means—

    (a) in relation to a magistrates' court in England and Wales, the designated officer for the court, and

    (b) in relation to any other court, the clerk of the court.

(8) If the holder of the licence has not caused it and its counterpart to be delivered, or has not posted them, in accordance with section 7 of this Act and does not produce the licence and counterpart as required under subsection (7) above, then he is guilty of an offence.

(9) Subsection (8) above does not apply to a person who—

    (a) satisfies the court that he has applied for a new licence and has not received it, or

    (b) surrenders to the court a current receipt for his licence and its counterpart issued under section 56 of this Act, and produces the licence and counterpart to the court immediately on their return.

(10) . . .

(11) ...

(12) Where on any occasion a court deals with an offender—

    (a) for an offence in respect of which an order was made under this section, or

    (b) for two or more offences in respect of any of which such an order was made, any period of disqualification which is on that occasion imposed under section 34 or 35 of this Act shall be treated as reduced by any period during which he was disqualified by reason only of an order made under this section in respect of any of those offences.

(13) Any reference in this or any other Act (including any Act passed after this Act) to the length of a period of disqualification shall, unless the context otherwise requires, be construed as a reference to its length before any reduction under this section.

When adjourning after conviction, or deferring sentence, the power to impose an interim disqualification applies to any offence carrying either obligatory or discretionary disqualification. Where obligatory, it will be the norm for the court to impose such a disqualification unless there is a good reason not to, for example where the defendant will be putting forward a special reason as to why he should not be disqualified. (See **Special reasons not to disqualify/ endorse**.) An interim disqualification is generally used now to prevent further similar offending during the period of an adjournment, rather than imposing a condition of bail not to drive. However, in some circumstances the court may impose both, particularly where if a defendant offends while on bail, consideration ought to be given to revoking his bail. When imposing an interim disqualification, the court does not specify any length of time for such an order. An interim disqualification will automatically cease to have effect at the end of six months, beginning with the day on which it was imposed, unless it ends earlier.[4] No further order of interim disqualification can be made for the same offence, or for offences in respect of which an interim order could have been made at the time the first order was made.[5] However, this does not prevent an offence for which the defendant is convicted subsequent to the first order being made from being the subject of a further interim order.

An interim disqualification order does not revoke the driving licence, and the court does not have the power to order such a disqualification to be endorsed on the licence. Failure to produce a driving licence to the court following the making of an order of interim disqualification is an offence under s.26(8) of the Act. This offence is summary only. Penalties for the offence are set out in Sch.2 of the Road Traffic Offenders Act 1988 (see **Appendix 2**).

An interim disqualification may also be imposed when committing for sentence under s.6 of the Powers of the Criminal Courts (Sentencing) Act 2000.

---

[4] s.26(4).
[5] s.26(6).

No such order may be made when committing for trial. The court retains power to impose a condition of bail not to drive, but such a condition should only be imposed before conviction where there are grounds under the Bail Act 1976 to justify its imposition, and it will not cause injustice.[6]

[6] *R. v Kwame* [1975] R.T.R. 106.

Disqualification, Obligatory and Discretionary, Orders for

(Reference: Wilkinson's Road Traffic Offences, Ch.20.)

The court's powers to disqualify are set out in ss.34, 35 and 36 of the Road Traffic Offenders Act 1988.

Section 34 deals with the power to disqualify in relation to the offence. For some offences the power to disqualify will be obligatory, in others discretionary. (See Table of Endorsable Offences in **Appendix 1**.)

34 Disqualification for Certain Offences

(1) Where a person is convicted of an offence involving obligatory disqualification, the court must order him to be disqualified for such period not less than twelve months as the court thinks fit unless the court for special reasons thinks fit to order him to be disqualified for a shorter period or not to order him to be disqualified.

(1A) Where a person is convicted of an offence under section 12A of the Theft Act 1968 (aggravated vehicle-taking), the fact that he did not drive the vehicle in question at any particular time or at all shall not be regarded as a special reason for the purposes of subsection (1) above.

(2) Where a person is convicted of an offence involving discretionary disqualification, and either—

(a) the penalty points to be taken into account on that occasion number fewer than twelve, or

(b) the offence is not one involving obligatory endorsement,

the court may order him to be disqualified for such period as the court thinks fit.

(3) Where a person convicted of an offence under any of the following provisions of the Road Traffic Act 1988, that is—

(aa) section 3A (causing death by careless driving when under the influence of drink or drugs),

(a) section 4(1) (driving or attempting to drive while unfit),

(b) section 5(1)(a) (driving or attempting to drive with excess alcohol), . . .

(c) section 7(6) (failing to provide a specimen) where that is an offence involving obligatory disqualification,

(d) section 7A(6) (failing to allow a specimen to be subjected to laboratory test) where that is an offence involving obligatory disqualification, has within the ten years immediately preceding the commission of the offence been convicted of any such offence, subsection (1) above shall apply in relation to him as if the reference to twelve months were a reference to three years.

(4) Subject to subsection (3) above, subsection (1) above shall apply as if the reference to twelve months were a reference to two years—

    (a) in relation to a person convicted of—

        (i) manslaughter, or in Scotland culpable homicide, or

        (ii) an offence under section 1 of the Road Traffic Act 1988 (causing death by dangerous driving), or

        (iii) an offence under section 3A of that Act (causing death by careless driving while under the influence of drink or drugs), and

    (b) in relation to a person on whom more than one disqualification for a fixed period of 56 days or more has been imposed within the three years immediately preceding the commission of the offence.

(4A) For the purposes of subsection (4)(b) above there shall be disregarded any disqualification imposed under section 26 of this Act or section 147 of the Powers of Criminal Courts (Sentencing) Act 2000 or section 223A or 436A of the Criminal Procedure (Scotland) Act 1975 (offences committed by using vehicles) and any disqualification imposed in respect of an offence of stealing a motor vehicle, an offence under section 12 or 25 of the Theft Act 1968, an offence under section 178 of the Road Traffic Act 1988, or an attempt to commit such an offence.

(4B) Where a person convicted of an offence under section 40A of the Road Traffic Act 1988 (using vehicle in dangerous condition etc) has within the three years immediately preceding the commission of the offence been convicted of any such offence, subsection (1) above shall apply in relation to him as if the reference to twelve months were a reference to six months.

(5) The preceding provisions of this section shall apply in relation to a conviction of an offence committed by aiding, abetting, counseling or procuring, or inciting to the commission of, an offence involving obligatory disqualification as if the offence were an offence involving discretionary disqualification.

(6) This section is subject to section 48 of this Act.

Obligatory disqualification due to nature of offence

Where an offender is convicted of an offence carrying obligatory disqualification, the court must impose a disqualification of not less than 12 months.[1]

---

[1] s.34(1).

The minimum period of disqualification is increased to two years[2] where either:

1. an offender is convicted of:

   (a) manslaughter;

   (b) causing death by dangerous driving;

   (c) causing death by careless driving when under the influence of drink or drugs; or

2. an offender has had imposed more than one disqualification for a fixed period of 56 days or more, in the three years immediately preceding the commission of the offence. (Interim disqualifications and disqualifications for non-endorsable offences, e.g. taking a vehicle without consent, do not count.)

The minimum period of disqualification is increased to three years[3] for the following offences where an offender has previously been *convicted* (whether or not subsequently *disqualified*) of such an offence within the 10 years preceding the commission of this offence. The offences are:

(a) causing death by careless driving when under the influence of drink or drugs;

(b) driving or attempted driving when unfit through drink or drugs;

(c) driving or attempted driving above the prescribed alcohol limit;

(d) failing/refusing to provide an evidential specimen for analysis when the accused had been driving or attempting to drive.

For certain offences, the court has the power to make an order reducing the period of the obligatory disqualification (which can reduce the period below the statutory minimum) provided the offender completes a specified course designed to prevent future offending.

The Road Traffic Offenders Act 1988 s.34A:

34A   REDUCED DISQUALIFICATION PERIOD FOR ATTENDANCE ON COURSES

(1) This section applies where—

   (a) a person is convicted of an offence under section 3A (causing death by careless driving when under influence of drink or drugs), 4 (driving or being in charge when under influence of drink or drugs), 5 (driving or being in charge with excess alcohol) or 7 (failing to provide a specimen) of the Road Traffic Act 1988, and

---

[2] s.34(4).
[3] s.34(3).

(b) the court makes an order under section 34 of this Act disqualifying him for a period of not less than twelve months.

(2) Where this section applies, the court may make an order that the period of disqualification imposed under section 34 shall be reduced if, by a date specified in the order under this section, the offender satisfactorily completes a course approved by the Secretary of State for the purposes of this section and specified in the order.

(3) The reduction made by an order under this section in a period of disqualification imposed under section 34 shall be a period specified in the order of not less than three months and not more than one quarter of the unreduced period (and accordingly where the period imposed under section 34 is twelve months, the reduced period shall be nine months).

(4) The court shall not make an order under this section unless—

(a) it is satisfied that a place on the course specified in the order will be available for the offender,

(b) the offender appears to the court to be of or over the age of 17,

(c) the court has explained the effect of the order to the offender in ordinary language, and has informed him of the amount of the fees for the course and of the requirement that he must pay them before beginning the course, and

(d) the offender has agreed that the order should be made.

(5) The date specified in an order under this section as the latest date for completion of a course must be at least two months before the last day of the period of disqualification as reduced by the order.

(6) An order under this section shall name the petty sessions area (or in Scotland the sheriff court district or, where an order has been made under this section by a stipendiary magistrate, the commission area) in which the offender resides or will reside.

Whether to make such an order, and if so, the period of reduction, is a matter for the discretion of the court. There is no entitlement to an order under this section, although courts will usually consider making such an order. However, there may be circumstances where the court may think that an order is not appropriate, for example where an offender has already attended such a course but has re-offended.

The reduction offered may not be less than three months or greater than one quarter of the unreduced period of disqualification.

The making of such an order requires the consent of the offender. Courts are tending to be flexible, and may be prepared to make the order in circumstances where the offender is unsure if he will take up a place on the course, rather than not offer it. There is no penalty for subsequently failing to complete the course; if the offender declines to participate, the obligatory disqualification imposed simply remains unreduced.

The course is educative and most suitable for those likely to respond by modifying their behaviour as a result of participating in the course. For this reason, it is generally thought to be less suitable for those who are suffering from a serious alcohol addiction who require a different form of intervention.

An offender can escape the requirements of an obligatory disqualification for the offence if he can establish special reasons, in which case the court may either not disqualify at all, or disqualify for a shorter period than the minimum required. (See **Special reasons not to disqualify/endorse**.)

Obligatory disqualification for repeated offences under the penalty points procedure

(See **Table of Endorsable Offences** in **Appendix 1**.)

The Road Traffic Offenders Act 1988 s.35:

35 DISQUALIFICATION FOR REPEATED OFFENCES

(1) Where—

(a) a person is convicted of an offence to which this subsection applies, and

(b) the penalty points to be taken into account on the occasion number twelve or more,

the court must order him to be disqualified for not less than the minimum period unless the court is satisfied, having regard to all the circumstances, that there are grounds for mitigating the normal consequences of the conviction and thinks fit to order him to be disqualified for a shorter period or not to order him to be disqualified.

(1A) Subsection (1) above applies to—

(a) an offence involving discretionary disqualification and obligatory endorsement, and

(b) an offence involving obligatory disqualification in respect of which no order is made under section 34 of this Act.

(2) The minimum period referred to in subsection (1) above is—

(a) six months if no previous disqualification imposed on the offender is to be taken into account, and

(b) one year if one, and two years if more than one, such disqualification is to be taken into account;

and a previous disqualification imposed on an offender is to be taken into account if it was for a fixed period of 56 days or more and was imposed within the three years immediately preceding the commission of the latest offence in respect of which penalty points are taken into account under section 29 of this Act.

(3) Where an offender is convicted on the same occasion of more than one offence to which subsection (1) above applies—

(a) not more than one disqualification shall be imposed on him under subsection (1) above,

(b) in determining the period of the disqualification the court must take into account all the offences, and

(c) for the purposes of any appeal any disqualification imposed under subsection (1) above shall be treated as an order made on the conviction of each of the offences.

(4) No account is to be taken under subsection (1) above of any of the following circumstances—

(a) any circumstances that are alleged to make the offence or any of the offences not a serious one,

(b) hardship, other than exceptional hardship, or

(c) any circumstances which, within the three years immediately preceding the conviction, have been taken into account under that subsection in ordering the offender to be disqualified for a shorter period or not ordering him to be disqualified.

(5) References in this section to disqualification do not include a disqualification imposed under section 26 of this Act or section 147 of the Powers of Criminal Courts (Sentencing) Act 2000 or section 223A or 436A of the Criminal Procedure (Scotland) Act 1975 (offences committed by using vehicles) or a disqualification imposed in respect of an offence of stealing a motor vehicle, an offence under section 12 or 25 of the Theft Act 1968, an offence under section 178 of the Road Traffic Act 1988, or an attempt to commit such an offence.

(5A) The preceding provisions of this section shall apply in relation to a conviction of an offence committed by aiding, abetting, counseling, procuring, or inciting to the commission of, an offence involving obligatory disqualification as if the offence were an offence involving discretionary disqualification.

(6) . . .

(7) This section is subject to section 48 of this Act.

This form of disqualification is referred to as a "penalty points" disqualification, or a "totting up" disqualification. It is obligatory and can only be avoided if the court finds "mitigating circumstances".[4] (See **Special reasons not to disqualify/endorse** and **Mitigating circumstances**.)

The penalty points to be taken into account on conviction, for the purpose of determining whether a penalty points disqualification should be imposed, are set out in s.29 of the Road Traffic Offenders Act.

---

[4] Road Traffic Offenders Act 1988 s.35(4).

29   Penalty Points to be Taken into Account on Conviction

(1) Where a person is convicted of an offence involving obligatory endorsement, the penalty points to be taken into account on that occasion are (subject to subsection (2) below)—

   (a) any that are to be attributed to the offence or offences of which he is convicted, disregarding any offence in respect of which an order under section 34 of this Act is made, and

   (b) any that were on a previous occasion ordered to be endorsed on the counterpart of any licence held by him, unless the offender has since that occasion and before the conviction been disqualified under section 35 of this Act.

(2) If any of the offences was committed more than three years before another, the penalty points in respect of that offence shall not be added to those in respect of the other.

12 penalty points, or more, to be taken into account will require a court to impose a disqualification under s.35. In determining how many points to take into account, s.29(1)(a) specifically exempts from consideration offences of which an offender is convicted for which the court has determined to make an order for either obligatory or discretionary disqualification under s.34 of the Act. Thus, if such an order is not made, then those offences must have points attributed to them, to be taken into consideration. However, s.34(2) (see above) only allows a discretionary disqualification to be imposed for an offence where the penalty points to be taken into account on that occasion number fewer than 12.

The legislation is undoubtedly circular; whether the court has power to disqualify as a matter of discretion depends upon the penalty points to be taken into account, but the number of points to be taken into account depends on whether or not the court exercises its discretion to disqualify.

This dilemma has been resolved to an extent by the case of *Jones v DPP* [2001] R.T.R. 80. Where a penalty points disqualification will apply, if the court does not disqualify for the offence under s.34(2), the proper approach for the court is to consider first whether to impose a discretionary disqualification under s.34(2), but in the light of the defendant's whole record; if the court concludes that there should be a longer disqualification because of his record, then a disqualification under s.35 should be imposed. This preserves the ability of the court to make a short order of disqualification for the offence under s.34(2), where justified in the light of the offender's record, the effect of which will avoid a disqualification under s.35 being imposed. Of course, if the offence itself does not merit disqualification, the offender must still be disqualified under s.35. Although this might appear to be an anomalous situation, a penalty points disqualification, unlike any other type of disqualification, will remove from the defendant's licence any previous penalty points endorsed. An offender who escapes a penalty points disqualification due to a discretionary disqualification being imposed for the offence remains liable to such a disqualification in the future, as the penalty points which put him at risk remain on his licence, whereas the offender who has received the penalty points disqualification has a "clean" licence in terms of future offences.

The statutory period of disqualification is a *minimum* period of six months. The court may impose a longer period. The minimum period increases where there are qualifying previous orders of disqualification to be taken into account.[5] One previous disqualification for 56 days or more will increase the minimum period to one year, two such previous disqualifications increase the minimum to two years. To qualify, the disqualifications must have been imposed in the three years immediately preceding the commission of the offence.

The court can only impose one disqualification under s.35(1), regardless of how many offences are before the court. However, in fixing the period of disqualification, all the offences should be taken into account,[6] as should the number of penalty points that will be wiped off by reason of the disqualification and also the points that would be incurred but for the disqualification. A court must distinguish between offenders when imposing such orders.

---

[5] s.35(2).
[6] s.35(3).

Discretionary disqualification

A discretionary disqualification may be imposed for any endorsable offence, or for non-endorsable offences where statutory provisions permit,[1] for any period.

A disqualification of 56 days or more will result in any licence issued under the 1988 Act being revoked. (See **Revocation of Licence**.)

Unlike a penalty point disqualification, a discretionary disqualification does not result in the removal from the defendant's licence of any previously endorsed penalty points.

A discretionary disqualification may still be considered even where, in the absence of such a disqualification, the number of points required to be endorsed will lead to an obligatory "totting" or penalty points disqualification.[2] (See **Obligatory disqualification for repeated offences under the penalty points procedure**.) The court should first consider whether to exercise its discretionary power to disqualify. If, having decided so to disqualify, the length of that disqualification would match or exceed an obligatory penalty point disqualification, the court should impose the penalty point disqualification thus giving the defendant the benefit of the effect of such a disqualification in removing previous points from the licence.

A person who commits an offence that does not require obligatory endorsement but other statutory powers permit a sentence to include an order for disqualification, e.g. taking a motor vehicle without consent, may be disqualified under this section, although such a conviction can never trigger a penalty points disqualification.

Whether or not to impose a discretionary disqualification, and if so the length of that order, is always a matter for the court. That discretion should be exercised judicially, taking into account the nature and circumstances of the offence(s) and the offenders record.[3] The magistrates courts guidelines give guidance on when courts should be considering disqualification for offences.

---

[1] See, for example, s.147 Powers of Criminal Courts (Sentencing) Act 2000 which allows courts to impose a driving disqualification where a vehicle has been used for criminal purposes.

[2] *Jones v DPP* [2001] R.T.R. 80.

[3] *R v Squires* [2007] EWCA Crim 2391, the main purpose of disqualification was forward-looking and preventative rather than backward-looking and punitive, and shorter bans would be appropriate where the offender had a good driving record before the offence and where the offence had resulted from a momentary error of judgment.

Requirement to produce driving licence

The requirement to produce a licence applies on conviction for an offence involving obligatory or discretionary disqualification. Failure to produce the licence as required by the Act is an offence, and any licence is automatically suspended until so produced.

The Road Traffic Offenders Act s.27:

27 PRODUCTION OF LICENCE

(1) Where a person who is the holder of a licence is convicted of an offence involving obligatory or discretionary disqualification, and a court proposes to make an order disqualifying him or an order under section 44 of this Act, the court must, unless it has already received them, require the licence and its counterpart to be produced to it.

(2) . . .

(3) If the holder of the licence has not caused it and its counterpart to be delivered, or posted it and its counterpart, in accordance with section 7 of this Act and does not produce it and its counterpart as required under this section or section 40 of the Crime (Sentences) Act 1997, section 146 or 147 of the Powers of Criminal Courts (Sentencing) Act 2000 or section 223A or 436A of the Criminal Procedure (Scotland) Act 1975, or if the holder of the licence does not produce it and its counterpart as required by section 40B of the Child Support Act 1991, then, unless he satisfies the court that he has applied for a new licence and has not received it—

    (a) he is guilty of an offence, and

    (b) the licence shall be suspended from the time when its production was required until it and its counterpart are produced to the court and shall, while suspended, be of no effect.

(4) Subsection (3) above does not apply where the holder of the licence—

    (a) has caused a current receipt for the licence and its counterpart issued under section 56 of this Act to be delivered to the proper officer of the court not later than the day before the date appointed for the hearing, or

    (b) has posted such a receipt, at such time that in the ordinary course of post it would be delivered not later than that day, in a letter duly addressed to the proper officer and either registered or sent by the recorded delivery service, or

    (c) surrenders such a receipt to the court at the hearing,

and produces the licence and its counterpart to the court immediately on their return.

(5) . . .

Disqualification until test is passed

The Road Traffic Offenders Act 1988 s.36 sets out the circumstances in which a court must impose a disqualification until a test is passed, and the circumstances when it may do so.

36   Disqualification Until Test is Passed

(1) Where this subsection applies to a person the court must order him to be disqualified until he passes the appropriate driving test.

(2) Subsection (1) above applies to a person who is disqualified under section 34 of this Act on conviction of—

   (a) manslaughter, or in Scotland culpable homicide, by the driver of a motor vehicle, or
   (b) an offence under section 1 (causing death by dangerous driving) or section 2 (dangerous driving) of the Road Traffic Act 1988.

(3) . . .

(4) Where a person to whom subsection (1) above does not apply is convicted of an offence involving obligatory endorsement, the court may order him to be disqualified until he passes the appropriate driving test (whether or not he has previously passed any test).

(5) In this section—

   "appropriate driving test" means—

   (a) an extended driving test, where a person is convicted of an offence involving obligatory disqualification or is disqualified under section 35 of this Act,
   (b) a test of competence to drive, other than an extended driving test, in any other case,

   "extended driving test" means a test of competence to drive prescribed for the purposes of this section, and

   "test of competence to drive" means a test prescribed by virtue of section 89(3) of the Road Traffic Act 1988.

(6) In determining whether to make an order under subsection (4) above, the court shall have regard to the safety of road users.

(7) Where a person is disqualified until he passes the extended driving test—

   (a) any earlier order under this section shall cease to have effect, and
   (b) a court shall not make a further order under this section while he is so disqualified.

(8) Subject to subsection (9) below, a disqualification by virtue of an order under this section shall be deemed to have expired on production to the Secretary of State of evidence, in such form as may be prescribed by regulations under section 105 of the Road Traffic Act 1988, that the person disqualified has passed the test in question since the order was made.

(9) A disqualification shall be deemed to have expired only in relation to vehicles of such classes as may be prescribed in relation to the test passed by regulations under that section.

(10) Where there is issued to a person a licence on the counterpart of which are endorsed particulars of a disqualification under this section, there shall also be endorsed the particulars of any test of competence to drive that he has passed since the order of disqualification was made.

In addition to the power to disqualify for the offence, and under the penalty points procedure, the court also has power to impose a disqualification until a driving test is passed, where an offender is convicted of any endorsable offence.[1]

In deciding whether to make such an order, the court must have regard to the safety of other road users.[2] The purpose of such an order is to be treated as a road safety measure, rather than punitive, and should be considered in cases where the circumstances of the offence or the offender are such that it is in the public interest that the offender be submitted to a driving test before being allowed to drive unsupervised on the road. In certain circumstances (see s.36(1) above) such a disqualification is obligatory.

The test will normally be the standard driving test. Where an offender is convicted of an offence carrying obligatory disqualification under s.34 or is disqualified under s.35 of the Act, the test that the offender is required to pass before the disqualification is lifted will be an extended test. An order to complete an extended test will revoke any earlier order under s.36, and while such an order remains, no further order can be made under the section.

An order under s.36 will not apply until any other order for obligatory or discretionary disqualification has come to an end. When the order takes effect, the offender may not drive until he has obtained a provisional licence and he must comply with the conditions of that licence. If he fails to do so, and drives, he will be committing an offence of driving while disqualified.[3]

---

[1] s.36(4).
[2] s.36(6).
[3] Road Traffic Act 1988 s.103.

Disqualification, Application to remove

The Road Traffic Offenders Act s.42 sets out the circumstances in which a person may apply to the court to have an order for disqualification removed.

42   REMOVAL OF DISQUALIFICATION

(1) Subject to the provisions of this section, a person who by an order of a court is disqualified may apply to the court by which the order was made to remove the disqualification.

(2) On any such application the court may, as it thinks proper having regard to—

    (a) the character of the person disqualified and his conduct subsequent to the order,

    (b) the nature of the offence, and

    (c) any other circumstances of the case,

either by order remove the disqualification as from such date as may be specified in the order or refuse the application.

(3) No application shall be made under subsection (1) above for the removal of a disqualification before the expiration of whichever is relevant of the following periods from the date of the order by which the disqualification was imposed, that is—

    (a) two years, if the disqualification is for less than four years,

    (b) one half of the period of disqualification, if it is for less than ten years but not less than four years,

    (c) five years in any other case;

and in determining the expiration of the period after which under this subsection a person may apply for the removal of a disqualification, any time after the conviction during which the disqualification was suspended or he was not disqualified shall be disregarded.

(4) Where an application under subsection (1) above is refused, a further application under that subsection shall not be entertained if made within three months after the date of the refusal.

(5) If under this section a court orders a disqualification to be removed, the court—

    (a) must cause particulars of the order to be endorsed on the counterpart of the licence, if any, previously held by the applicant, and

    (b) may in any case order the applicant to pay the whole or any part of the costs of the application.

(5A) Subsection (5)(a) above shall apply only where the disqualification was imposed in respect of an offence involving obligatory endorsement; and in any other case the court must send notice of the order made under this section to the Secretary of State.

(5B) A notice under subsection (5A) above must be sent in such manner and to such address, and must contain such particulars, as the Secretary of State may determine.

(6) The preceding provisions of this section shall not apply where the disqualification was imposed by order under section 36(1) of this Act.

Application is by way of complaint to the court acting for the area which made the original order of disqualification and for a summons to be issued to the chief officer of police to show cause why the order applied for should not be made.[1] If the original disqualification was varied by the Crown Court on appeal, it is submitted that application should still be made to the magistrates' court that made the order subsequently varied.

The court may order the removal of any driving disqualification imposed by it, with the exception of a disqualification until a test is passed imposed under s.36(1) of the Road Traffic Offenders Act 1988.[2] This restriction does not prevent the court from removing any other disqualification imposed under a different section, leaving unaltered the disqualification until a test is passed. It would appear that disqualifications imposed under s.147 of the Powers of Criminal Courts Sentencing Act 2000 (using a vehicle for criminal purposes) may be removed under this section.

The effect of s.42(3) is to prevent any application in respect of a disqualification of two years or less.

Application may be made, regardless of whether the disqualification was mandatory or discretionary. However, a court may be less ready to remove a mandatory disqualification.[3] The court may grant the application to take effect immediately, or from a specified date. A decision to revoke from a future date will not prevent a further application from being made before that specified date for immediate removal.[4]

If an application is successful, the order for removal will be endorsed on the counterpart of any licence previously held, or notice sent to the Secretary of State if the order is made in respect of a non-endorsable offence. In addition, the court may order a successful applicant to pay the whole or any part of the costs of the application.[5] Presumably an unsuccessful applicant or respondent may also be ordered to pay costs under the general power to award costs following the determination of an application on complaint.[6]

---

[1] CPR 2005 r.55.2.
[2] s.42(6).
[3] *Damer v Davison* [1976] R.T.R. 44.
[4] *R. v Manchester JJ. Ex p. Gaynor* [1956] 1 All E.R. 610. Subject to the provisions of s.42(4).
[5] s.42(5).
[6] Magistrates' Courts Act 1980 s.64.

Where an application made under s.42(1) of the Act is refused, no further application may be made within three months after the date of refusal.[7]

---

[7] s.42(4).

Driver/Driving, Meaning of

(Reference: Wilkinson's Road Traffic Offences, Ch.1.)

"Driving" does not have a statutory definition. Case law has provided a number of examples of what amounts to driving, some of them conflicting. The judgement of Lord Widgery C.J. in *R. v McDonagh* [1974] R.T.R 372 suggests that it is essentially a question of fact, dependent on the degree and extent to which the person has control of the direction and movement of the vehicle. A person cannot be said to be driving unless they are "in a substantial sense controlling the movement and direction of the car". However, even if this test is met, it still has to be considered whether the activity falls within the ordinary meaning of the word "driving". "The essence of driving is the use of the driver's controls in order to direct the movement, however that movement is produced."[1]

The following are examples of what has been held to amount to driving, and what has not.

> A person who pushed a car along a road with both feet on the ground, controlling the steering wheel was not driving.[2]

> A person sat in the driver's seat of a car that had no keys in the ignition, the steering wheel locked and the engine not running was "driving" when the car was allowed to roll a distance of 30ft by gravity and the handbrake then applied.[3]

---

[1] *Whitfield v DPP* [1998] Crim. L.R. 349.
[2] *R v McDonagh* [1974] R.T.R. 372.
[3] *Burgoyne v Phillips* [1983] R.T.R. 49.

Driving while disqualified for holding or obtaining a licence

(Reference: Wilkinson's Road Traffic Offences, Ch.11.)

The Road Traffic Act 1988 s.103 creates offences of driving whilst disqualified, or attempting to obtain a licence while disqualified.

103   OBTAINING LICENCE, OR DRIVING, WHILE DISQUALIFIED

(1) A person is guilty of an offence if, while disqualified for holding or obtaining a licence, he

  (a) obtains a licence, or
  (b) drives a motor vehicle on a road.

(2) A licence obtained by a person who is disqualified is of no effect (or, where the disqualification relates only to vehicles of a particular class, is of no effect in relation to vehicles of that class).

(3) [repealed]

(4) Subsection (1) above does not apply in relation to disqualification by virtue of section 101 of this Act.

(5) Subsection (1)(b) above does not apply in relation to disqualification by virtue of section 102 of this Act.

(6) In the application of subsection (1) above to a person whose disqualification is limited to the driving of motor vehicles of a particular class by virtue of—

  (a) section 102, 117 or 117A of this Act, or
  (b) subsection (9) of section 36 of the Road Traffic Offenders Act 1988 (disqualification until test is passed),

the references to disqualification for holding or obtaining a licence and driving motor vehicles are references to disqualification for holding or obtaining a licence to drive and driving motor vehicles of that class.

An offence is committed under this section either by driving a motor vehicle in breach of an order for disqualification, or by obtaining a licence in breach of an order for disqualification. Where the offence is committed by driving, it applies to a motor vehicle, and the driving must take place on a road.

The offence is one of strict liability. Only the fact of the disqualification need be proved; lack of knowledge of the disqualification will not afford a defence. However, the fact of disqualification must be proved and to the criminal standard. Not only must the prosecution prove beyond reasonable doubt that an order for disqualification was made, and the period covered by the order, but that the person against whom the order was made is the defendant. Proving the fact of disqualification may therefore sometimes cause evidential difficulties, usually in terms of sufficiency of evidence to prove the identity of the person previously disqualified. There are a number of ways in which proof may be adduced and the three methods identified in the case of *R. v Derwentside JJ. Ex p. Heaviside* [1996] R.T.R. 384 (admission, fingerprints, or direct evidence from someone present in court at the time) are not exhaustive.[1] Normally it will be sufficient that the details on the memorandum of conviction match those of the defendant, and in the absence of any contradictory evidence, that will be sufficient evidence upon which the court can rely. Proof can be by any admissible means, including a non-formal admission.[2]

In extreme circumstances, the defence of necessity from duress could arise, but only if the accused could be said to be acting reasonably and proportionately in order to avoid a death or serious injury.[3]

A defendant who drives while subject to an order disqualifying him until a test is passed under s.36 of the Road Traffic Offenders Act 1988 will commit an offence under s.103(1)(b) if he fails to comply with the conditions of any licence issued to him before he has passed the appropriate re-test. The burden of showing that he is not driving in breach of such conditions is on the defendant.[4]

A person will be committing an offence under s.103(1)(b) if at the time he drives, he is subject to a driving disqualification, even if the order is subsequently set aside on appeal,[5] or he makes a statutory declaration that has the effect of voiding the original order.

---

[1] *R. v Derwentside Magistrates' Court Ex p. Swift; R. v Sunderland Magistrates' Court Ex p. Bate* [1997] R.T.R. 89.
[2] *Pattison v DPP* [2005] EWHC 2938; (2006) 170 J.P. 51, in which there is an extensive review of the authorities.
[3] *R. v Martin* [1989] R.T.R. 63.
[4] *DPP v Barker* [2004] EWHC 2502; (2004) 168 J.P. 617.
[5] *R. v Lynn* [1977] R.T.R. 369.

Offence	Mode of trial	Section	Imprisonment	Level of fine	Disqualification	Penalty points	Endorsement code	Sentencing guidelines
Obtaining driving licence whilst disqualified	Summary	s.103(1)(a)	—	3		—	—	—
Driving whilst disqualified	Summary	s.103(1)(b)	6 months or level 5 or both		Discretionary	6	BA10	Consider community order, custody [Fine Band C]

Drive whilst disqualified	Road Traffic Act 1988, s.103

Triable only summarily:
Maximum penalty: Level 5 fine and/or 6 months

Must endorse and may disqualify. If no disqualification, impose 6 points

OFFENCE SERIOUSNESS (CULPABILITY AND HARM)
A. IDENTIFY THE APPROPRIATE STARTING POINT
Starting points based on first time offender* pleading not guilty

Examples of nature of activity	Starting point	Range
Full period expired but retest not taken	Low level community order	Band C fine to medium level community order 6 points or disqualify for 3 – 6 months
Lengthy period of ban already served	High level community order	Medium level community order to 12 weeks custody Lengthen disqualification for 6 – 12 months beyond expiry of current ban
Recently imposed ban	12 weeks custody	High level community order to 26 weeks custody Lengthen disqualification for 12 – 18 months beyond expiry of current ban

OFFENCE SERIOUSNESS (CULPABILITY AND HARM)
B. CONSIDER THE EFFECT OF AGGRAVATING AND MITIGATING FACTORS
(OTHER THAN THOSE WITHIN EXAMPLES ABOVE)
Common aggravating and mitigating factors are identified in the pullout card. The following may be particularly relevant but these lists are not exhaustive:

Factors indicating higher culpability	Factors indicating lower culpability
1. Never passed test 2. Planned long-term evasion 3. Vehicle obtained during ban 4. Driving for remuneration Factors indicating greater degree of harm 1. Distance driven 2. Evidence of associated bad driving 3. Offender caused accident	1. Defendant not present when disqualification imposed and genuine reason why unaware of ban 2. Genuine emergency established

FORM A PRELIMINARY VIEW OF THE APPROPRIATE SENTENCE, THEN CONSIDER OFFENDER MITIGATION
Common factors are identified in the pullout card

CONSIDER A REDUCTION FOR GUILTY PLEA

CONSIDER ANCILLARY ORDERS, INCLUDING DEPRIVATION OF PROPERTY
Refer to pages 142-148 for guidance on available ancillary orders

DECIDE SENTENCE

GIVE REASONS

Note

An offender convicted of this offence will always have at least one relevant previous conviction for the offence that resulted in disqualification. The starting points and ranges take this into account; any other previous convictions should be considered in the usual way – see page 3.

Driving while disqualified by reason of age

The Road Traffic Act 1988, s.101:

101 DISQUALIFICATION OF PERSONS UNDER AGE

(1) A person is disqualified for holding or obtaining a licence to drive a motor vehicle of a class specified in the following Table if he is under the age specified in relation to it in the second column of the Table.

TABLE

Class of motor vehicle	Age (in years)
1. Invalid carriage	16
2. Moped	16
3. Motor bicycle	17
4. Agricultural or forestry tractor	17
5. Small vehicle	17
6. Medium-sized goods vehicle	18
7. Other motor vehicles	21

Note that this section does not create an offence. Further, s.103(4) of the Road Traffic Act 1988 specifically excludes under-age drivers from the provisions of that section. Under-age drivers must therefore be charged with driving without a licence contrary to s.87 of the Road Traffic Act 1988 if they drive a motor vehicle on a road.

Driving whilst unfit/over the permitted limit—Generally

(Reference: Wilkinson's Road Traffic Offences, Ch.4.)

There are two main types of offences commonly referred to as "drink-driving" offences:

a) driving, attempting to drive, or being in charge of a mechanically propelled vehicle whilst unfit through drink or drugs (s.4 of the Road Traffic Act 1988);

b) driving, attempting to drive, or being in charge of a motor vehicle over the permitted alcohol limit (s.5 of the Road Traffic Act 1988).

Between them, the two sections of the Act create six separate offences. The charge must be clear as to which of the offences is alleged.

All offences under these sections must be committed on a road or other public place. The required elements of the offences relating to unfitness, drink or drugs are closely linked under the two sections, but have significantly different requirements in terms of what must be proved.

The offence under s.4 may be committed in relation to drink or drugs, whereas the offence under s.5 is specifically a drink related offence. The offence under s.5 simply requires proof that the amount of alcohol exceeded the prescribed limit, whereas under s.4 proof of impairment to drive through consumption of alcohol (or drugs) is required. In the case of drink related offences, it has become increasingly common to charge the offence under s.5 where there is an evidential specimen that can be relied upon, but to lay an alternative charge under s.4 in the event of a challenge to the procedure which led to the provision of the specimen, or the reliability of the specimen. In such circumstances, the prosecution will not normally seek a conviction in relation to both offences.

Issues relating to lawfulness of arrest for these offences are irrelevant as there is no requirement for an arrest. Even where a preliminary screening test proves negative, a defendant may still be arrested for the purpose of obtaining an evidential specimen and any such specimen provided should not be excluded as unfairly obtained.[1]

The defence of duress may, in appropriate circumstances, be available for these offences; insanity will not be as no *mens rea* is required, the offences being of strict liability.

There is a statutory defence available to offences of being "in charge",[2] where a defendant can prove that at the material time the circumstances were such that there was no likelihood of his driving so long as he remained unfit to drive

---

[1] *DPP v Robertson* [2002] EWHC 542; [2002] R.T.R. 22.
[2] See s.4(3) and s.5(2) of the Road Traffic Act 1988.

through drink or drugs, or exceeded the prescribed limit. In determining such a likelihood the court may disregard any injury to him or any damage to the vehicle.[3] The burden of proof is on the defendant, and it is a legal burden to be discharged to the balance of probabilities.[4]

Further related offences are created by s.6(6) and s.7(6) of the Road Traffic Act 1998, where a person fails without a reasonable excuse to provide a preliminary or an evidential specimen for analysis, or refuses to allow laboratory analysis of a specimen taken under s.7A of the Act.

---

[3] See s.4(4) and s.5(3) of the Road Traffic Act 1988.
[4] *Sheldrake v DPP* [2005] R.T.R. 2, and see also *CPS v Bate* [2004] EWHC 2811.

Offence	Mode of trial	Section	Imprison- ment	Fine	Disqualifica- tion	Penalty Points	Endorsement code
Driving or attempting to drive when unfit through drink or drugs	Summarily	4(1)	6 months	Level 5	Obligatory	3–11	DR20 drink DR80 drugs
Being in charge of a mechan- ically propelled vehicle when unfit through drink or drugs	Summarily	4(2)	3 months	Level 4	Discretion- ary	10	DR50 drink DR90 drugs
Driving or attempting to drive with excess alcohol in breath, blood or urine	Summarily	5(1)	6 months	Level 5	Obligatory	3–11	DR10
Being in charge of a motor vehicle with excess alcohol in breath, blood or urine	Summarily	5(2)	3 months	Level 4	Discretion- ary	10	DR40

Offence	Mode of trial	Section	Imprisonment	Fine	Disqualifica-tion	Penalty Points	Endorsement code
Failing to co-operate with a preliminary test	Summarily	6(6)	No	Level 3	Discretion-ary	4	DR70
Failing to provide specimen for analysis or laboratory test	Summarily	7(6)	6 months if defendant driving or attempting to drive	Level 5	Obligatory	3–11	DR30
			3 months in all other cases	Level 4	Discretion-ary	10	DR60
Failing to allow specimen to be subject to laboratory test	Summarily	7A(6)	6 months if defendant driving or attempting to drive	Level 5	Obligatory	3–11	—
			3 months in all other cases	Level 4	Discretion-ary	10	—

Preliminary and evidential specimens

Preliminary tests (which are merely indicative of a possible offence) must be distinguished from evidential tests (which are required to prove the offence). Section 6 of the Road Traffic Act 1988 sets out the power to administer preliminary tests. There are three types of preliminary test; the preliminary breath test under s.6A,[1] a preliminary impairment test under s.6B and a preliminary drugs test under s.6C. (For the tests under s.6B and s.6C, see **Driving whilst unfit through drink or drugs**.) The statutory requirements that must be fulfilled before a constable may require a person to co-operate with any one or more of the tests are the same for all three types of test. Section 6(6) makes it an offence to fail to co-operate with a preliminary test without a reasonable excuse. (See **Failing to provide a specimen**.)

The Road Traffic Act s.6:

6 POWER TO ADMINISTER PRELIMINARY TESTS

(1) If any of subsections (2) to (5) applies a constable may require a person to co-operate with any one or more preliminary tests administered to the person by that constable or another constable.

(2) This subsection applies if a constable reasonably suspects that the person—

   (a) is driving, is attempting to drive or is in charge of a motor vehicle on a road or other public place, and

   (b) has alcohol or a drug in his body or is under the influence of a drug.

(3) This subsection applies if a constable reasonably suspects that the person—

   (a) has been driving, attempting to drive or in charge of a motor vehicle on a road or other public place while having alcohol or a drug in his body or while unfit to drive because of a drug, and

   (b) still has alcohol or a drug in his body or is still under the influence of a drug.

(4) This subsection applies if a constable reasonably suspects that the person—

   (a) is or has been driving, attempting to drive or in charge of a motor vehicle on a road or other public place, and

---

[1] There is no requirement on the prosecution to adduce in evidence the result of a preliminary breath test in figures. The roadside breath test, as s.6A of the Road Traffic Act provided, was a procedure by which an indication of whether the prescribed limit was likely to be exceeded was obtained, and the specimen had no greater status. See *Smith v DPP* [2007] EWHC 100 (Admin).

(b) has committed a traffic offence while the vehicle was in motion.

(5) This subsection applies if—

(a) an accident occurs owing to the presence of a motor vehicle on a road or other public place, and

(b) a constable reasonably believes that the person was driving, attempting to drive or in charge of the vehicle at the time of the accident.

(6) A person commits an offence if without reasonable excuse he fails to co-operate with a preliminary test in pursuance of a requirement imposed under this section.

(7) A constable may administer a preliminary test by virtue of any of subsections (2) to (4) only if he is in uniform.

(8) In this section—

(a) a reference to a preliminary test is to any of the tests described in sections 6A to 6C, and

(b) "traffic offence" means an offence under—

(i) a provision of Part II of the Public Passenger Vehicles Act 1981 (c 14),

(ii) a provision of the Road Traffic Regulation Act 1984 (c 27),

(iii) a provision of the Road Traffic Offenders Act 1988 (c 53) other than a provision of Part III, or

(iv) a provision of this Act other than a provision of Part V.

6A Preliminary Breath Test

(1) A preliminary breath test is a procedure whereby the person to whom the test is administered provides a specimen of breath to be used for the purpose of obtaining, by means of a device of a type approved by the Secretary of State, an indication whether the proportion of alcohol in the person's breath or blood is likely to exceed the prescribed limit.

(2) A preliminary breath test administered in reliance on section 6(2) to (4) may be administered only at or near the place where the requirement to co-operate with the test is imposed.

(3) A preliminary breath test administered in reliance on section 6(5) may be administered—

(a) at or near the place where the requirement to co-operate with the test is imposed, or

(b) if the constable who imposes the requirement thinks it expedient, at a police station specified by him.

Driving, or being in charge whilst unfit through drink or drugs

The Road Traffic Act s.4:

4   DRIVING, OR BEING IN CHARGE, WHEN UNDER INFLUENCE OF DRINK OR DRUGS

(1) A person who, when driving or attempting to drive a mechanically propelled vehicle on a road or other public place, is unfit to drive through drink or drugs is guilty of an offence.

(2) Without prejudice to subsection (1) above, a person who, when in charge of a mechanically propelled vehicle which is on a road or other public place, is unfit to drive through drink or drugs is guilty of an offence.

(3) For the purposes of subsection (2) above, a person shall be deemed not to have been in charge of a mechanically propelled vehicle if he proves that at the material time the circumstances were such that there was no likelihood of his driving it so long as he remained unfit to drive through drink or drugs.

(4) The court may, in determining whether there was such likelihood as is mentioned in subsection (3) above, disregard any injury to him and any damage to the vehicle.

(5) For the purposes of this section, a person shall be taken to be unfit to drive if his ability to drive properly is for the time being impaired.

An offence under s.4 is committed by driving, attempting to drive, or being in charge of a mechanically propelled vehicle on a road or other public place, whilst unfit through drink or drugs.

Under s.4(5) a person shall be taken as "unfit to drive" if his ability to drive properly is for the time being impaired. Evidence of impairment may be as to the manner of the defendant's driving (erratic, an accident in circumstances where there is no obvious hazard), or the state of the defendant (falling asleep, unable to stand up, mental confusion). To establish impairment, the prosecutor need only show that the defendant could not drive properly. This will usually be in the form of some sort of expert opinion evidence from a police doctor, but lack of such evidence is not fatal.[1] Evidence of the results of any preliminary

---

[1] *Leetham v DPP* [1999] R.T.R. 29: a conviction was upheld based on fast and erratic driving, admitted consumption of cannabis confirmed by blood analysis, the known effects of the drug and the evidence of officers who stopped him that his eyes were red and glazed and that his speech was slow and slurred.

impairment test may also be given. A witness who has no particular expertise other than being a driver may not give evidence as to impairment. An inference of impairment can also be drawn from high blood alcohol content.

Preliminary impairment tests

The preliminary impairment test is now a statutory test under s.6B of the Road Traffic Act 1988.

6B   PRELIMINARY IMPAIRMENT TEST

(1) A preliminary impairment test is a procedure whereby the constable administering the test—

(a) observes the person to whom the test is administered in his performance of tasks specified by the constable, and

(b) makes such other observations of the person's physical state as the constable thinks expedient.

(2) The Secretary of State shall issue (and may from time to time revise) a code of practice about—

(a) the kind of task that may be specified for the purpose of a preliminary impairment test,

(b) the kind of observation of physical state that may be made in the course of a preliminary impairment test,

(c) the manner in which a preliminary impairment test should be administered, and

(d) the inferences that may be drawn from observations made in the course of a preliminary impairment test.

(3) In issuing or revising the code of practice the Secretary of State shall aim to ensure that a preliminary impairment test is designed to indicate—

(a) whether a person is unfit to drive, and

(b) if he is, whether or not his unfitness is likely to be due to drink or drugs.

(4) A preliminary impairment test may be administered—

(a) at or near the place where the requirement to co-operate with the test is imposed, or

(b) if the constable who imposes the requirement thinks it expedient, at a police station specified by him.

(5) A constable administering a preliminary impairment test shall have regard to the code of practice under this section.

(6) A constable may administer a preliminary impairment test only if he is approved for that purpose by the chief officer of the police force to which he belongs.

(7) A code of practice under this section may include provision about—

    (a) the giving of approval under subsection (6), and

    (b) in particular, the kind of training that a constable should have undergone, or the kind of qualification that a constable should possess, before being approved under that subsection.

The specific tests to be undertaken are set out in a pro forma (MG DD/F) and the Code of Practice for the Preliminary Impairment Tests[2] applies. The tests are:

a) the Romberg test;

b) the walk and turn test;

c) the one leg stand test; and

d) the finger and nose test.

The police officer administering such a test must be approved for the purpose. The pro forma enjoins the officer to give a warning that the results of the test may be given in evidence.

A preliminary test for drugs has also recently been introduced as a statutory preliminary test under s.6C of the Road Traffic Act 1988 (see below).

There must be evidence that the impairment is the result of drink or drugs. Evidence of the results of any preliminary impairment test may also be given. A witness who has no particular expertise other than being a driver may not give evidence as to impairment. An inference of impairment can also be drawn from high blood alcohol content. Evidence of analysis of any specimen of blood, breath or urine, must be taken into account.[3] The only exception will be where the court excludes such evidence as unfairly obtained.[4]

Drugs

A "drug" includes any intoxicant other than alcohol.[5] It is suggested that an intoxicant is any substance that affects the self-control of the human body. Any drug is capable of causing an offence under s.4, provided it leads to impairment to drive, it is irrelevant whether it is an illegal substance, or prescribed medicine, or otherwise. However, the prosecutor must show a causal link between the affect of the drug and the impairment.

Section 6C of the Road Traffic Act 1988 has introduced a statutory preliminary test for drugs, which can be administered using an approved device.

---

[2] Issued by the Department for Transport in December 2004.
[3] Road Traffic Offenders Act 1988 s.15(2).
[4] Police and Criminal Evidence Act 1984 s.78.
[5] Road Traffic Act 1988 s.11(2).

6C   PRELIMINARY DRUG TEST

(1) A preliminary drug test is a procedure by which a specimen of sweat or saliva is—

(a) obtained, and

(b) used for the purpose of obtaining, by means of a device of a type approved by the Secretary of State, an indication whether the person to whom the test is administered has a drug in his body.

(2) A preliminary drug test may be administered—

(a) at or near the place where the requirement to co-operate with the test is imposed, or

(b) if the constable who imposes the requirement thinks it expedient, at a police station specified by him.

For the purpose of furthering an investigation into whether an offence has been committed under s.4, a police officer may require provision of an evidential specimen under s.7 of the Road Traffic Act 1988. (See **Preliminary and evidential specimens** and **Failing to provide a specimen**.)

Section 7(3)(bc) specifically enables a constable to require a specimen of blood or urine following a positive preliminary drug test. This new section overcomes the previous difficulty caused by the legislation where such a specimen could not be required at a police station unless the reasons for not requiring a breath specimen applied. Alternatively, such a specimen may be required following the advice of a medical practitioner that the condition of the person might be due to some drug.[6] The fact that a breath specimen has already been given is irrelevant.

Unlike alcohol specimens, testing is to establish the presence of drugs (or not) within the body, and results are not directly referable to likely levels of impairment. There is no statutory assumption that the amount of drug in the analysed specimen is not less than at the time of the offence. Presumably it is open to a defendant to challenge the certificate on the basis of post-driving "drug" consumption. Issues may also arise as to the effect of the drug on capability to drive where drugs may have been consumed days prior to testing but residues remain.

---

[6] It is necessary at the time of provision of the blood specimen for there to have been a clear oral statement at the police station by the doctor to the effect that he believed that drugs were a possible cause of the defendant's condition; *Cole v DPP* [1988] R.T.R. 224.

Unfit through drink or drugs (drive/attempt to drive)	Road Traffic Act 1988, s.4(1)

Triable only summarily:
Maximum penalty: Level 5 fine and/or 6 months

- Must endorse and disqualify for at least 12 months
- Must disqualify for **at least** 2 years if offender has had two or more disqualifications for periods of 56 days or more in preceding 3 years – **refer to page 159 and consult your legal adviser for further guidance**
- Must disqualify for **at least** 3 years if offender has been convicted of a relevant offence in preceding 10 years – **refer to page 159 and consult your legal adviser for further guidance.**

If there is a delay in sentencing after conviction, consider interim disqualification

Note: the final column below provides guidance regarding the length of disqualification that may be appropriate in cases to which the 3 year minimum applies. The period to be imposed in any individual case will depend on an assessment of all the relevant circumstances, including the length of time since the earlier ban was imposed and the gravity of the current offence.

OFFENCE SERIOUSNESS (CULPABILITY AND HARM)
A. IDENTIFY THE APPROPRIATE STARTING POINT
Starting points based on first time offender pleading not guilty

Examples of nature of activity	Starting point	Range	Disqualification	Disqual. 2nd offence in 10 years
Evidence of moderate level of impairment and no aggravating factors	Band C fine	Band C fine	12 – 16 months	36 – 40 months
Evidence of moderate level of impairment and presence of one or more aggravating factors listed below	Band C fine	Band C fine	17 – 22 months	36 – 46 months
Evidence of high level of impairment and no aggravating factors	Medium level community order	Low level community order to high level community order	23 – 28 months	36 – 52 months
Evidence of high level of impairment and presence of one or more aggravating factors listed below	12 weeks custody	High level community order to 26 weeks custody	29 – 36 months	36 – 60 months

OFFENCE SERIOUSNESS (CULPABILITY AND HARM)
B. CONSIDER THE EFFECT OF AGGRAVATING AND MITIGATING FACTORS (OTHER THAN THOSE WITHIN EXAMPLES ABOVE)
Common aggravating and mitigating factors are identified in the pullout card. The following may be particularly relevant but these lists are not exhaustive:

Factors indicating higher culpability	Factors indicating lower culpability
1. LGV, HGV, PSV etc.	1. Genuine emergency established *
2. Poor road or weather conditions	2. Spiked drinks *
3. Carrying passengers	3. Very short distance driven *
4. Driving for hire or reward	
5. Evidence of unacceptable standard of driving	* even where not amounting to special reasons
Factors indicating greater degree of harm	
1. Involved in accident	
2. Location e.g. near school	
3. High level of traffic or pedestrians in the vicinity	

FORM A PRELIMINARY VIEW OF THE APPROPRIATE SENTENCE, THEN CONSIDER OFFENDER MITIGATION
Common factors are identified in the pullout card

CONSIDER A REDUCTION FOR GUILTY PLEA

CONSIDER OFFERING DRINK/DRIVE REHABILITATION COURSE

CONSIDER ANCILLARY ORDERS
Refer to pages 142-148 for guidance on available ancillary orders

DECIDE SENTENCE

GIVE REASONS

Unfit through drink or drugs (in charge)	Road Traffic Act 1988, s.4(2)

Triable only summarily:
Maximum penalty: Level 4 fine and/or 3 months

Must endorse and may disqualify. If no disqualification, impose 10 points

OFFENCE SERIOUSNESS (CULPABILITY AND HARM)		
A. IDENTIFY THE APPROPRIATE STARTING POINT		
Starting points based on first time offender pleading not guilty		
Examples of nature of activity	**Starting point**	**Range**
Evidence of moderate level of impairment and no aggravating factors	Band B fine	Band B fine 10 points
Evidence of moderate level of impairment and presence of one or more aggravating factors listed below	Band B fine	Band B fine 10 points or consider disqualification
Evidence of high level of impairment and no aggravating factors	Band C fine	Band C fine to medium level community order 10 points or consider disqualification
Evidence of high level of impairment and presence of one or more aggravating factors listed below	High level community order	Medium level community order to 12 weeks custody Consider disqualification OR 10 points

OFFENCE SERIOUSNESS (CULPABILITY AND HARM)	
B. CONSIDER THE EFFECT OF AGGRAVATING AND MITIGATING FACTORS	
(OTHER THAN THOSE WITHIN EXAMPLES ABOVE)	
Common aggravating and mitigating factors are identified in the pullout card. The following may be particularly relevant but these lists are not exhaustive:	
Factors indicating higher culpability	Factor indicating lower culpability
1. LGV, HGV, PSV etc. 2. High likelihood of driving 3. Driving for hire or reward	1. Low likelihood of driving

FORM A PRELIMINARY VIEW OF THE APPROPRIATE SENTENCE, THEN CONSIDER OFFENDER MITIGATION
Common factors are identified in the pullout card

CONSIDER A REDUCTION FOR GUILTY PLEA

CONSIDER ANCILLARY ORDERS
Refer to pages 142-148 for guidance on available ancillary orders

DECIDE SENTENCE

GIVE REASONS

Driving, or attempting to drive over the prescribed limit

The Road Traffic Act 1988 s.5 creates offences of driving, attempting to drive or being in charge when over the prescribed limit.

5 DRIVING OR BEING IN CHARGE OF A MOTOR VEHICLE WITH ALCOHOL CONCENTRATION ABOVE PRESCRIBED LIMIT

(1) If a person—

    (a) drives or attempts to drive a motor vehicle on a road or other public place, or

    (b) is in charge of a motor vehicle on a road or other public place,

after consuming so much alcohol that the proportion of it in his breath, blood or urine exceeds the prescribed limit he is guilty of an offence.

(2) It is a defence for a person charged with an offence under subsection (1)(b) above to prove that at the time he is alleged to have committed the offence the circumstances were such that there was no likelihood of his driving the vehicle whilst the proportion of alcohol in his breath, blood or urine remained likely to exceed the prescribed limit.

(3) The court may, in determining whether there was such a likelihood as is mentioned in subsection (2) above, disregard any injury to him and any damage to the vehicle.

These offences are committed by driving, attempting to drive, or being in charge of a motor vehicle on a road or other public place after consuming so much alcohol that the amount in breath, blood or urine exceeds the prescribed limit.

The prescribed limit[1] is:

    a) $35\mu g$ of alcohol in 100 ml of breath;

    b) 80mg of alcohol in 100ml of blood;

    c) 107mg of alcohol in 100ml of urine.

The statute does not require the prosecution to prove exactly how much alcohol is present in breath, blood or urine, only that the amount present exceeds the permitted limit.[2]

The alcohol is required to have been "consumed", but this does not mean it has to have been drunk; entry into the body other than by mouth is included.[3]

---

[1] Road Traffic Act 1988 s.11(2).

[2] *Gordon v Thorpe* [1986] Crim. L.R. 61.

[3] *DPP v Johnson (David)* [1995] R.T.R. 9, alcohol injected was "consumed", a purposeful interpretation of the legislation.

The meaning of "breath" is not restricted to deep lung air and the word should be given its ordinary dictionary meaning "air exhaled from any thing", see *Zafar v DPP* [2004] EWHC 2468; [2005] R.T.R. 18. The significance of the decision in *Zafar* is that it prevents a defendant from arguing that the breath reading is inaccurate due to contamination from residual mouth alcohol or due to alcohol vapour present in the upper respiratory tract as a result of gastro-oesophageal reflux or alcohol otherwise "brought up" from the stomach (although modern breathalyser machines are designed to analyse deep lung air as it provides a more accurate indicator of the amount of alcohol circulating in the blood). Although the presence of alcohol in breath from such occurrences cannot be used as a challenge to the reliability of the reading and afford a defence to the charge, it is capable of amounting to a special reason.[4] The court will need to be convinced of the fact of such a matter before finding such a special reason exists. Expert opinion will almost certainly be required.

For details of the requirement to provide a specimen for analysis see **Failing to provide a specimen for analysis**.

Analysis of a specimen of blood or urine must be by an approved analyst.

There is an irrebuttable statutory assumption that the amount of alcohol present at the time of driving was not less than the amount of alcohol present in the analysed sample.[5]

The only circumstance where this assumption does not apply is where a defendant can prove that he consumed alcohol before he provided the specimen and after he had ceased to drive, attempt to drive, or be in charge of the vehicle, and that had he not done so, the proportion of alcohol would not have exceeded the prescribed limit. (Note that it is only open to a defendant to lead evidence of post offence consumption where the reduction in the level of the reading would bring it below the prescribed limit. It does not appear possible to call such evidence to mitigate the seriousness of an offence by seeking to reduce a high reading.) (See further **Back calculations**.)

---

[4] *Ng v DPP* [2006] EWHC 56 (Admin).
[5] s.15(2), Road Traffic Offenders Act 1988. This provision does not breach a defendant's human rights; *Griffiths v DPP* [2002] EWHC 792; (2002) 166 J.P. 629.

Excess alcohol (drive/attempt to drive)	Road Traffic Act 1988, s ⁊ ⁊)

Triable only summarily:
Maximum penalty: Level 5 fine and/or 6 months

- Must endorse and disqualify for at least 12 months
- Must disqualify for **at least** 2 years if offender has had two or more disqualifications for ⁊s of 56 days or more in preceding 3 years – **refer to page 159 and consult your legal adviser for f⁊ ⁊ guidance**
- Must disqualify for **at least** 3 years if offender has been convicted of a relevant offenc⁊ ⁊eceding 10 years – **refer to page 159 and consult your legal adviser for further guidance**.

If there is a delay in sentencing after conviction, consider interim disqualificatio⁊

Note: the final column below provides guidance regarding the length of disqualifica⁊ ⁊t may be appropriate in cases to which the 3 year minimum applies. The period to be imposed in any indi⁊ ⁊case will depend on an assessment of all the relevant circumstances, including the length of time since ⁊ ⁊ier ban was imposed and the gravity of the current offence.

OFFENCE SERIOUSNESS (CULPAB⁊ AND HARM)
A. IDENTIFY THE APPROPRIAT⁊ ARTING POINT
Starting points based on first time offend⁊ ⁊ading not guilty

Level of alcohol Breath (mg)	Blood (ml)	Urine (ml)	Starting point	Range	Disqualification	Disqual. 2nd offence in 10 years – see note above
36 – 59	81-137	108-183	Band C fine	Bar⁊ ⁊e	12 – 16 months	36 – 40 months
60 – 89	138-206	184-274	Band C fine	F⁊ ⁊fine	17 – 22 months	36 – 46 months
90 – 119	207-275	275-366	Medium level community order	⁊level ⁊mmunity order ⁊ high level community order	23 – 28 months	36 – 52 months
120 – 150 and above	276-345 and above	367-459 and above	12 weeks custody	High level community order to 26 weeks custody	29 – 36 months	36 – 60 months

OFFENCE SF⁊ ⁊JSNESS (CULPABILITY AND HARM)
B. CONSIDER THE EF⁊ ⁊ OF AGGRAVATING AND MITIGATING FACTORS (OTHER T⁊ ⁊ THOSE WITHIN EXAMPLES ABOVE)
Common aggravating and mitiga⁊ ⁊actors are identified in the pullout card. The following may be particularly relevant but ⁊ ⁊ lists are not exhaustive:

Factors indicating higher culpability	Factors indicating lower culpability
1. LGV, HGV, PSV etc.	1. Genuine emergency established *
2. Poor road or weather conditions	2. Spiked drinks *
3. Carrying passengers	3. Very short distance driven *
4. Driving for hire or reward	
5. Evidence of unacceptable st⁊ ⁊d of driving	* even where not amounting to special reasons

Factors indicating greater d⁊ ⁊of harm
1. Involved in accident
2. Location e.g. near sch⁊
3. High level of traffic or ⁊trians in the vicinity

FORM A PRELIM⁊ ⁊Y VIEW OF THE APPROPRIATE SENTENCE, THEN CONSIDER OFFENDER MI⁊ ⁊TION
Common facto⁊ ⁊e identified in the pullout card

CONSIDER A REDUCTION FOR GUILTY PLEA

CONSID⁊ ⁊FFERING DRINK/DRIVE REHABILITATION COURSE

CONS⁊ ⁊R ANCILLARY ORDERS, INCLUDING FORFEITURE OR SUSPENSION OF PE⁊ ⁊AL LIQUOR LICENCE
Re⁊ ⁊ pages 142-148 for guidance on available ancillary orders

DECIDE SENTENCE

GIVE REASONS

Excess alcohol (in charge)	Road Traffic Act 1988, s.5(1)(b)

Triable only summarily:
Maximum penalty: Level 4 fine and/or 3 months

Must endorse and may disqualify. If no disqualification, impose 10 points

OFFENCE SERIOUSNESS (CULPABILITY AND HARM)
A. IDENTIFY THE APPROPRIATE STARTING POINT
Starting points based on first time offender pleading not guilty

Level of alcohol Breath (mg)	Blood (ml)	Urine (ml)	Starting point	Range
36 – 59	81-137	108-183	Band B fine	Band B fine 10 points
60 – 89	138-206	184-274	Band B fine	Band B fine 10 points OR consider disqualification
90 – 119	207-275	275-366	Band C fine	Band C fine to medium level community order Consider disqualification up to 6 months OR 10 points
120 – 150 and above	276-345 and above	367-459 and above	Medium level community order	Low level community order to 6 weeks custody Disqualify 6-12 months

OFFENCE SERIOUSNESS (CULPABILITY AND HARM)
B. CONSIDER THE EFFECT OF AGGRAVATING AND MITIGATING FACTORS (OTHER THAN THOSE WITHIN EXAMPLES ABOVE)
Common aggravating and mitigating factors are identified in the pullout card. The following may be particularly relevant but these lists are not exhaustive:

Factors indicating higher culpability	Factor indicating lower culpability
1. LGV, HGV, PSV etc.	1. Low likelihood of driving
2. Ability to drive seriously impaired	
3. High likelihood of driving	
4. Driving for hire or reward	

FORM A PRELIMINARY VIEW OF THE APPROPRIATE SENTENCE, THEN CONSIDER OFFENDER MITIGATION
Common factors are identified in the pullout card

CONSIDER A REDUCTION FOR GUILTY PLEA

CONSIDER ANCILLARY ORDERS, INCLUDING FORFEITURE OR SUSPENSION OF PERSONAL LIQUOR LICENCE
Refer to pages 142-148 for guidance on available ancillary orders

DECIDE SENTENCE

GIVE REASONS

Requirement to provide a specimen and the offence of failing to provide

Section 6 of the Road Traffic Act 1988 sets out the circumstances in which a person may be required to comply with a *preliminary* test. These tests are not evidential specimens, but act as "screening" tests to assist a constable in deciding whether to require an evidential specimen. It is not mandatory that a preliminary test has been required before an evidential specimen is sought. Section 6(6) creates the offence of failing to provide such a specimen. There is no statutory requirement to warn a person that failure to provide may lead to prosecution. However, an officer may arrest a person who fails such a test, or fails to co-operate with such a test.[1] See **Preliminary and evidential specimens**.

Section 7 of the Road Traffic Act 1988 sets out the circumstances in which a person may be required to provide an *evidential* specimen for analysis.[2] Section 7(6) creates the offence of failing to provide such a specimen. Section 7(7) imposes a duty on a police officer to warn that failure to provide a specimen may lead to prosecution.

7   PROVISION OF SPECIMENS FOR ANALYSIS

(1) In the course of an investigation into whether a person has committed an offence under section 3A, 4 or 5 of this Act a constable may, subject to the following provisions of this section and section 9 of this Act, require him—

(a) to provide two specimens of breath for analysis by means of a device of a type approved by the Secretary of State, or

(b) to provide a specimen of blood or urine for a laboratory test.

(2) A requirement under this section to provide specimens of breath can only be made—

(a) at a police station,

(b) at a hospital, or

(c) at or near a place where a relevant breath test has been administered to the person concerned or would have been so administered but for his failure to co-operate with it.

(2A) For the purposes of this section "a relevant breath test" is a procedure involving the provision by the person concerned of a specimen of breath to be used for the purpose of obtaining an indication whether the

---

[1] Road Traffic Act 1988 s.6D.

[2] Note that there are amendments to the legislation to allow evidential specimens to be taken at the roadside, once approval is given to appropriate devices for this purpose.

proportion of alcohol in his breath or blood is likely to exceed the prescribed limit.

(2B) A requirement under this section to provide specimens of breath may not be made at or near a place mentioned in subsection (2)(c) above unless the constable making it—

(a) is in uniform, or

(b) has imposed a requirement on the person concerned to co-operate with a relevant breath test in circumstances in which section 6(5) of this Act applies.

(2C) Where a constable has imposed a requirement on the person concerned to co-operate with a relevant breath test at any place, he is entitled to remain at or near that place in order to impose on him there a requirement under this section.

(2D) If a requirement under subsection (1)(a) above has been made at a place other than at a police station, such a requirement may subsequently be made at a police station if (but only if)—

(a) a device or a reliable device of the type mentioned in subsection (1)(a) above was not available at that place or it was for any other reason not practicable to use such a device there, or

(b) the constable who made the previous requirement has reasonable cause to believe that the device used there has not produced a reliable indication of the proportion of alcohol in the breath of the person concerned.

(3) A requirement under this section to provide a specimen of blood or urine can only be made at a police station or at a hospital; and it cannot be made at a police station unless—

(a) the constable making the requirement has reasonable cause to believe that for medical reasons a specimen of breath cannot be provided or should not be required, or

(b) specimens of breath have not been provided elsewhere and at the time the requirement is made a device or a reliable device of the type mentioned in subsection (1)(a) above is not available at the police station or it is then for any other reason not practicable to use such a device there, or

(bb) a device of the type mentioned in subsection (1)(a) above has been used (at the police station or elsewhere) but the constable who required the specimens of breath has reasonable cause to believe that the device has not produced a reliable indication of the proportion of alcohol in the breath of the person concerned, or

(bc) as a result of the administration of a preliminary drug test, the constable making the requirement has reasonable cause to believe that the person required to provide a specimen of blood or urine has a drug in his body, or

(c) the suspected offence is one under section 3A or 4 of this Act and the constable making the requirement has been advised by a medical practitioner that the condition of the person required to provide the specimen might be due to some drug;

but may then be made notwithstanding that the person required to provide the specimen has already provided or been required to provide two specimens of breath.

(4) If the provision of a specimen other than a specimen of breath may be required in pursuance of this section the question whether it is to be a specimen of blood or a specimen of urine and, in the case of a specimen of blood, the question who is to be asked to take it shall be decided (subject to subsection (4A)) by the constable making the requirement.

(4A) Where a constable decides for the purposes of subsection (4) to require the provision of a specimen of blood, there shall be no requirement to provide such a specimen if—

    (a) the medical practitioner who is asked to take the specimen is of the opinion that, for medical reasons, it cannot or should not be taken; or

    (b) the registered health care professional who is asked to take it is of that opinion and there is no contrary opinion from a medical practitioner;

and, where by virtue of this subsection there can be no requirement to provide a specimen of blood, the constable may require a specimen of urine instead.

(5) A specimen of urine shall be provided within one hour of the requirement for its provision being made and after the provision of a previous specimen of urine.

(6) A person who, without reasonable excuse, fails to provide a specimen when required to do so in pursuance of this section is guilty of an offence.

(7) A constable must, on requiring any person to provide a specimen in pursuance of this section, warn him that a failure to provide it may render him liable to prosecution.

A person can be lawfully required to provide a specimen under this section only in the course of an investigation into an offence under s.4 (Driving or being in charge, whilst unfit through drink or drugs) or under s.5 (Driving or being in charge, over the prescribed limit) of the Road Traffic Act 1988.

There is no requirement for the person to have been arrested and the legality of any arrest will not be an issue.[3] It is irrelevant whether such an offence has in fact been committed, provided there is a bona fide investigation in progress.[4]

A requirement to provide a specimen for analysis (i.e. an "evidential" specimen) can only be made by a constable. The constable need not be specially authorised or trained or in uniform.

---

[3] *Fox v Gwent Chief Constable* [1985] R.T.R. 337.
[4] *Pearson v Commissioner of Police of the Metropolis* [1988] R.T.R. 276.

A person may be required to provide a specimen of breath (two samples), blood, or urine (to be supplied within one hour of the requirement being made, and after a previous specimen has been provided).[5] At present, a sample of breath can only be required at a police station.[6]

At a police station, a constable is compelled to ask for a specimen of breath, rather than blood or urine unless one of five situations set out in s.7(3) exists:

(a) the constable has reasonable grounds to believe such a specimen cannot or should not be required for medical reasons (s.7(3)(a));

(b) device not available or unreliable or not practicable to use it (s.7(3)(b));

(c) device has been used but the constable has reasonable cause to believe it has produced an unreliable indication (s.7(3)(bb));

(d) positive preliminary drug test (s.7(3)(bc));

(e) the suspected offence is under ss.3A or 4 of the Act and a medical practitioner advises that the defendant's condition might be due to some drug (s.7(3)(c)).

Reasonable grounds to believe such a specimen cannot or should not be required for medical reasons

It is the officer making the requirement for an alternative specimen who must make the decision as to whether there are reasonable grounds for believing a breath specimen cannot or should not be required. That officer may consult others, usually a medical officer.[7] Mere suspicion is not sufficient. The test as to whether there are reasonable grounds for such a belief is an objective one, the fact that the officer himself did not hold such a belief is immaterial.[8] The reason for not being required to provide a breath sample must be a medical one. Self-induced intoxication is capable of amounting to such a medical reason.[9]

Device not available or unreliable or not practicable to use it

Section 7(3)(b) does not require an officer to immediately move to request an alternative sample of blood or urine. Where a machine is available but thought to be unreliable or it is not practicable to use it, the defendant may be taken to another police station to use another breathalyser machine,[10] but need not be.[11] The device must be unreliable at the time the request for the alternative

---

[5] Road Traffic Act 1988 s.7(5).
[6] Evidential specimens will be able to be taken at the roadside once type approval orders are in force for the new machines.
[7] *Horrocks v Binns* [1986] R.T.R. 202.
[8] *White v Proudlock* [1988] R.T.R.163.
[9] *Young v DPP* [1992] R.T.R. 328.
[10] *Denny v DPP* [1990] R.T.R. 417.
[11] *Chief Constable of Kent v Berry* [1986] Crim. L.R. 748.

specimen is made.[12] It is the officer who makes the requirement for an alternative specimen who must have cause to believe that there is no device available, or that a device is unreliable or it is not practicable to use it. A reliable device is one which the officer reasonably believes to be reliable.[13] There may be a variety of reasons why it is not practicable to use a device, including where there is no trained operator available.[14]

Device has been used but the constable has reasonable cause to believe it has produced an unreliable indication

This section was introduced as a result of the capability of the new breathalyser machines to identify and flag up automatically certain conditions, e.g. interfering substances, presence of mouth alcohol, or disparate readings where the machine will give an automatic indication of unreliability if the difference between the samples is considered too great (about 15 per cent). Whilst s.7(3)(bb) entitled a police officer to require a specimen of blood or urine in the event of an unreliable indication being obtained from breath specimens, nothing in the section stated that in such a case an officer was obliged to require blood or urine or that a further breath test could not be offered. In such a case where a police officer gave the defendant the choice of providing two further breath specimens, or giving blood, the further breath specimens obtained in the circumstances were admissible and could be relied upon.[15]

Positive preliminary drug test and medical practitioner advises defendant's condition might be due to some drug

These will only be applicable to offences under ss.3A or 4 of the Road Traffic Act. (See **Driving whilst unfit or being in charge whilst unfit through drink or drugs**.)

Where one of the grounds under s.7(3) exists and a breath specimen cannot be required, the defendant must be informed of that fact,[16] and warned that failure to supply an alternative specimen or blood or urine may result in prosecution.[17]

Requirement to provide a specimen of blood or urine

Where a specimen other than breath can be required by virtue of the provisions of s.7, it is not for the defendant to choose whether it will be blood or

---

[12] *Cotter v Kamil* [1984] R.T.R. 371; also *Oxford v Baxendale* [1986] Crim. L.R. 631 where breath specimens had been provided some time earlier, but it was later discovered that the machine was not operating reliably. At the time the request for blood was made, no reliable machine was available.

[13] *Thompson v Thynne* [1986] Crim. L.R. 629; *Badkin v Chief Constable of South Yorkshire* [1988] R.T.R. 401.

[14] *Chief Constable of Avon and Somerset Constabulary v Kelliher* [1986] Crim. L.R. 645.

[15] *Stewart v DPP* [2003] EWHC 1323; [2003] R.T.R. 35.

[16] This information need not be given by the officer conducting the procedure; *Bobin v DPP* [1999] R.T.R. 375.

[17] *DPP v Jackson; Stanley v DPP* [1998] R.T.R. 397.

urine, the choice is that of the constable alone.[18] There is no legal requirement to require blood, unless there is a medical reason otherwise.[19] However, if the officer intends to require the defendant to provide a specimen of blood, the defendant must be asked whether there are medical reasons, to be determined by a doctor,[20] why such a specimen could not or should not be taken from him.[21] If the doctor decides there are medical reasons for not taking blood, a specimen of urine may be required instead.

A specimen of blood is only "provided" by a person if he consents to the taking of such a specimen from him, and the specimen is taken by a medical practitioner or, if it is taken in a police station, either by a medical practitioner or by a registered health care professional.[22]

The legislation does not specify who may take the specimen of urine, and such a sample is usually taken by a police officer. Where a defendant is required to provide a specimen of urine, he must provide that specimen within an hour of the requirement for a specimen being made,[23] and that means he must be given an opportunity to provide that specimen during that period.[24] A failure to provide within the hour will not render inadmissible a specimen obtained more than an hour later. The purpose of the section is to provide a finite time beyond which an officer need not wait, and if a specimen is not provided within that time, the defendant can be charged with failing to provide.[25]

When blood and urine samples are taken, if the defendant so requires[26] at the time the specimen is taken, the sample must be divided in to two parts and one of the parts offered to the defendant.[27] A failure to comply with this requirement will render any evidence of analysis of the specimen inadmissible.

With regard to breath specimens, the requirement is to provide a specimen for analysis by means of a device of a type approved by the Secretary of State. It is an essential element of the prosecution case to lead evidence not only as to the identity of the type of device used to obtain a sample, but that the device is of a type approved by the Secretary of State under the section.

Type approval of devices

The Secretary of State has approved certain devices for use under s.7 of the Road Traffic Act 1988, and issued the appropriate Approval Orders. Proof of the

---

[18] Road Traffic Act 1988 s.7(4).

[19] *Joseph v DPP* [2003] EWHC 3078; [2004] R.T.R. 21.

[20] A police officer must not usurp the role of the doctor in deciding on the validity of a medical reason; *Wade v DPP* [1996] R.T.R. 177. However, where the reason given is not a medical reason, the officer need not consult a doctor; *Kinsella v DPP* [2002] EWHC 545.

[21] *DPP v Warren* [1992] Crim. L.R. 200.

[22] Road Traffic Act 1988 s.11(3).

[23] Road Traffic Act 1988 s.7(5).

[24] *Robertson v DPP* [2004] EWHC 517; where the defendant had not been permitted to provide such a sample until 30 minutes after the requirement was made, and failed to provide the specimen within the one hour period.

[25] *DPP v Baldwin* [2000] R.T.R. 314.

[26] It is submitted that the officer is under no duty to inform a defendant that he is entitled to a sample, nor to provide a suitable container.

[27] Road Traffic Offenders Act 1988 s.15(5).

requirement that the device be of a type approved can be achieved by reference to the relevant order, or by a police officer or other witness giving evidence of such approval.

There has been a whole line of authorities dealing with appeals against drink driving convictions where it was sought to challenge convictions on the grounds that the device was not of the type approved, should not have been type approved, and has been modified such that it is no longer type approved. It is not the function of the court in such cases to consider whether the type of machine should have been approved by the Secretary of State.[28]

A challenge to type approval places an evidential burden on the defendant to raise the matter in issue. Mere assertion or speculation will not suffice; the defence must put some relevant evidence before the court.[29] Once sufficiently raised, it is then for the prosecution to prove, beyond reasonable doubt, that the machine is of a type approved.

Not every modification to a machine will take it out of type approval. The alteration is likely to have to be such that the description in the schedule to the order no longer applies to the device.[30]

Reliability

A defendant may challenge the admissibility of a specimen on the basis that the analysis is unreliable. This may be alleged to be due to malfunctioning of a machine in the case of breath specimens, or some procedural or other failure in the laboratory analysis of blood or urine samples. The statutory assumption contained in s.15(2) of the Road Traffic Offenders Act 1988 does not prevent a defendant from challenging the reliability of the reading. Before the assumption applies, the court must be satisfied that the analysis of the specimen is reliable. In the case of blood and urine, the defendant has his half of the sample, analysis of which can be used to challenge the reliability of the laboratory analysis.

With regard to breathalyser devices, there is a presumption that the machine is working properly, but that presumption can be challenged by relevant evidence. The machines themselves carry out a pre and post test calibration check, and purge themselves between test samples, the results of which will appear on the printout. The operator should check that a machine has properly self-calibrated before and after a test.

Defendants wishing to challenge the accuracy of a device have sought disclosure of documents such as machine logs, service repair reports, test records, even design records and circuit diagrams, etc. in the hope that they will

---

[28] *DPP v Brown; DPP v Texeira* [2001] EWHC Admin 931; a failure to detect mouth alcohol did not result in a machine no longer being of a type approved. *DPP v Memery* [2002] EWHC 1720; [2003] R.T.R. 18; it was not open to the court to consider whether the Secretary of State in approving devices had acted unlawfully and/or Wednesbury unreasonably.

[29] *Skinner v DPP* [2004] EWHC 2914; [2005] R.T.R. 17. In the absence of any evidence to suggest that the software installed in the machine was not that which it ought to have been, the version of software being specified in the approval order, it was permissible for a court to assume that the software in the device was correct.

[30] *Richardson v DPP* [2003] EWHC 359, Burnton J. obiter.

contain some evidence to assist their case. There is no procedure for "discovery" of documents in magistrates' courts and a witness summons should not be issued as a disguised attempt to obtain such discovery.[31] (See **Disclosure**.)

The evidence put before the court to raise in issue reliability must be relevant.[32]

Reliability can be challenged by leading evidence of the amount of alcohol said to have been consumed.[33] This will normally require some expert evidence. The prosecution may use any relevant evidence to rebut the defendant's assertion, including the result of a positive roadside breath test.[34]

The Road Traffic Act s.8:

8 CHOICE OF SPECIMENS OF BREATH

(1) Subject to subsection (2) below, of any two specimens of breath provided by any person in pursuance of section 7 of this Act that with the lower proportion of alcohol in the breath shall be used and the other shall be disregarded.

(2) If the specimen with the lower proportion of alcohol contains no more than 50 μg of alcohol in 100 ml of breath, the person who provided it may claim that it should be replaced by such specimen as may be required under section 7(4) of this Act and, if he then provides such a specimen, neither specimen of breath shall be used.

Where the requirement to provide a specimen of breath has been fully complied with, the machine will have analysed two samples of breath. The prosecutor may only rely upon the lower reading, the other being disregarded.[35]

Under s.8(2) of the Road Traffic Act 1988, where a specimen of breath has been provided which results in a reading of no more than 50 μg, the defendant may claim that it should be replaced with a specimen of blood or urine under s.7(4). If he is not informed of that option, or improper pressure is put on him not to exercise his option[36] he is entitled to be acquitted, the statutory procedures not having been followed.[37] If the defendant is for some reason unable, or unwilling, to understand the choice available to him, the breath test can still be relied upon.[38] For the procedure to be followed when requiring an

---

[31] *R. v Skegness Magistrates' Court Ex p. Cardy; R. v Manchester Crown Court Ex p. Williams* [1985] R.T.R. 49, reapplied and reaffirmed in *DPP v McKeown; DPP v Jones* [1997] R.T.R. 162.

[32] *DPP v Brown; DPP v Texeira* [2001] EWHC Admin 931; evidence that a machine did not always detect presence of mouth alcohol was irrelevant in circumstances where there was no evidence to support mouth alcohol being present.

[33] *Cracknell v Willis* [1988] R.T.R. 1.

[34] *Lafferty v DPP* [1995] Crim. L.R. 429.

[35] Road Traffic Act 1988 s.8(1).

[36] It is not improper pressure where a police officer asked by the defendant whether it would make any difference replied that it would "probably not": *Sharp v Spencer* [1987] Crim. L.R. 420.

[37] *Anderton v Lythgoe* [1985] R.T.R. 395; *Green v Lockhart* 1986 S.L.T. 11.

[38] *DPP v Poole* [1992] R.T.R. 177; *DPP v Berry* (1996) 160 J.P. 707.

alternative specimen under s.7(4) of the Road Traffic Act, see **Requirement to provide a specimen of blood or urine**, above.

Where under s.8, the defendant has claimed his right to have the breath specimen replaced with an alternative specimen of blood or urine, and complies with the requirement to provide such a sample, the prosecutor may not subsequently rely on the breath reading to prove an offence,[39] even if for some reason the replacement sample cannot be relied upon by the prosecutor.[40] Equally, the defendant may not challenge the procedure followed in obtaining the breath specimen,[41] or the reliability of the breathalyser reading in such circumstances.[42] Further, the breath reading cannot be relied upon to establish special reasons.[43]

Section 8 only renders a breath specimen inadmissible in circumstances where no replacement specimen is provided by the defendant.[44] If, having claimed his right to have the breath specimen replaced with an alternative specimen of blood or urine, he then refuses or fails (whether deliberately or through no fault of his own)[45] to provide such a specimen, he should be charged with the offence under s.5, and not prosecuted for an offence of failing to provide under s.7(6), since in such circumstances the original breath specimen can be used in evidence against him. For this reason, there is no necessity to warn of the risk of prosecution for failing to comply when requiring provision of the replacement specimen under s.7(4) when that requirement arises from an election by the defendant under s.8(2).

Failing to provide a specimen

If a preliminary or evidential specimen is actually provided, no offence will be made out, unless the specimen is insufficient to be tested. Section.11(3) of the Road Traffic Act 1988 requires a specimen of breath "to be provided in such a way as to enable the objective of the test or analysis to be satisfactorily achieved".[46] Case law has held similarly in relation to provision of urine.[47]

"Fail" includes "refuse".[48]

The offence may be charged where a refusal is given, even if the defendant then changes his mind. The circumstances surrounding the refusal and change of mind will need to be taken into account.

---

[39] Road Traffic Act 1988 s.8(2).
[40] *Archbold v Jones* [1985] Crim. L.R. 740.
[41] *Prince v DPP* [1996] Crim. L.R. 343; the obtaining of the breath specimen was merely a precondition for the obtaining of the blood specimen, and there was no need for evidence of correct calibration of the device to be given.
[42] *Branagan v DPP* [2000] R.T.R. 235 and *Wright v DPP* [2005] EWHC 1211. If the machine were unreliable, an alternative specimen could be required under s.7(3)(b) in any event.
[43] *Smith v Geraghty* [1986] R.T.R. 222.
[44] *Hague v DPP* [1997] R.T.R. 146.
[45] *DPP v Winstanley* [1993] R.T.R. 222; *Hayes v DPP* [1993] Crim. L.R. 966.
[46] Although the breathalyser machines operate to take two samples of breath "per cycle", there is no statutory requirement that the two samples be provided in the same cycle: *Mercer v DPP* [2004] R.T.R. 8. See also *DPP v Derwen* [2007] EWHC 337. The breath provided must be sufficient for the machine to analyse: *Rweikiza v DPP* [2008] EWHC 386 (Admin).
[47] *R. v Coward* [1976] R.T.R. 425 and *McDougall v MacPhail* 1990 S.L.T. 801.
[48] Road Traffic Act 1988 s.11(2).

Where a defendant has already provided an evidential specimen of breath, but it being 50 μg or less, opts to provide a specimen of blood or urine, if he then refuses or fails to provide such a specimen, he is not guilty of the offence of failing to provide under s.7(6). The original breath specimen can be used in evidence against him.

A defendant does not have a right to choose which type of specimen he will provide. Therefore if he refuses to provide the specimen required, but indicates a willingness to provide an alternative specimen, he is still guilty of the offence of failing to provide.

The offence is only committed if the failure or refusal is "without reasonable excuse". The defence must raise the matter in issue (an evidential burden applies),[49] following which the prosecution are required to disprove any reasonable excuse, beyond reasonable doubt.[50] Although it will be a question of fact for the court to determine whether a defendant had a reasonable excuse, what is capable of amounting to a reasonable excuse is a matter of law. A mistaken or genuine belief, such as a belief that he had not consumed alcohol, that he had not committed the offence being investigated, that he has a right to delay providing a specimen until he has had access to legal advice or time to read the PACE codes of practice,[51] is not capable of amounting to a reasonable excuse.

Mental capacity can amount to a reasonable excuse, but whether the court finds it is in fact a reasonable excuse will depend on the particular circumstances.

A reasonable excuse for failing to provide a specimen "must arise out of a physical or mental inability to provide one[52] or a substantial risk to health in its provision".[53] Fear of needles, or an "invincible repugnance" to giving blood may amount to a reasonable excuse, but the circumstances will normally need to be pretty extreme for a court to find a defendant thereby incapable of providing such a specimen.[54] Such an inability is more likely to be established in relation to a breath specimen where a defendant is able to demonstrate a physical inability to provide the sufficient continuous flow of breath required by the machine. In most cases, medical evidence will be required to support such an assertion. Further, the court must be satisfied that there is a causative link between the inability to provide and the failure, and should consider the facts carefully. For example, an asthmatic who sucks on the mouthpiece, having clearly been told to

---

[49] Mere assertion that there is a reasonable excuse is insufficient, the defence must introduce sufficient evidence, which may be done by cross examination or by calling evidence, before the prosecution are required to disprove it.
[50] *R v Harling* [1970] R.T.R. 441; *R. v Knightley* [1971] 2 All E.R. 1041; *McKeon v DPP* [2007] EWHC 3216 (Admin).
[51] *DPP v Billington* [1988] R.T.R. 231; *DPP v Whalley* [1991] R.T.R. 161; *DPP v Varley* [1999] Crim. L.R. 753; *DPP v Noe* [2000] R.T.R. 351; *Campbell v DPP* [2002] EWHC 1314; *Kennedy v DPP* [2002] EWHC 2297; *Kirkup v DPP* [2003] EWHC 2354; *Whitley v DPP* [2003] EWHC 2512; *R. (on the application of Forde) v DPP* [2004] EWHC 1156. From the number of cases rejecting such submissions, it should be clear that the Divisional Court is unlikely to view sympathetically any delaying tactics and rule them incapable of amounting to a reasonable excuse.
[52] An intense fear of seeing blood is insufficient reason, as the reason must relate to the taking of blood, not seeing it: *DPP v Mukandiwa* [2005] EWHC 2977.
[53] *R. v Lennard* [1973] R.T.R. 252.
[54] *R. v Harding* [1974] R.T.R. 325; *Alcock v Read* [1980] R.T.R. 71.

blow into it, cannot rely on a defence of inability to provide, where his inability was not the cause of the failure to provide.[55] A motorist is not legally required to inform an officer conducting a breath test of any medical conditions that might prevent then from providing sufficient breath for a specimen. However, a failure to do so might result in the court concluding as a matter of evidence that any medical excuse belatedly proffered was not acceptable and indicated a wilful failure to provide a specimen.[56]

There is no reasonable excuse of "doing my best".

A defendant must be able to understand what is required of him, and in a case of doubt, a police officer should provide language interpretation, or seek the views of a medical officer to counter such issues being raised at trial.[57] Self-induced intoxication cannot amount to a reasonable excuse for failure to provide a specimen.[58]

As the requirement to provide a breath specimen requires that two specimens be provided sufficient for analysis, if one specimen of breath is provided, but there is a refusal or failure to provide the second, the appropriate offence will be one of failing to provide. The reading obtained from analysis of the one specimen provided, although insufficient as an evidential specimen to found a charge under s.5, is admissible for other purposes, e.g. as evidence of the defendant having consumed some alcohol.

Failing to allow a specimen to be laboratory tested

In certain circumstances, a police officer may request a medical practitioner to take a sample of blood from a person, irrespective of whether that person consents. That specimen may not be analysed without the permission of the person from whom it was taken. Refusal to allow it to be analysed will constitute an offence under s.7A(6). As with the offence under s.7(6), a formal requirement to give permission must have been made, and the defendant warned that a failure to give that permission may result in a prosecution.

The Road Traffic Act 1988 s.7A:

7A SPECIMENS OF BLOOD TAKEN FROM PERSONS INCAPABLE OF CONSENTING

(1) A constable may make a request to a medical practitioner for him to take a specimen of blood from a person ("the person concerned") irrespective of whether that person consents if—

(a) that person is a person from whom the constable would (in the absence of any incapacity of that person and of any objection under section 9) be entitled under section 7 to require the provision of a specimen of blood for a laboratory test;

---

[55] *DPP v Furby* [2000] R.T.R. 181, conviction upheld where a defendant deliberately failed to blow into the machine properly, but would not have been able to provide a specimen in any event.
[56] *Piggott v DPP* [2008] EWHC 305 (Admin)
[57] *Chief Constable of Avon & Somerset v Singh* [1988] R.T.R. 107.
[58] *DPP v Beech* [1992] Crim. L.R. 64.

    (b) it appears to that constable that that person has been involved in an accident that constitutes or is comprised in the matter that is under investigation or the circumstances of that matter;

    (c) it appears to that constable that that person is or may be incapable (whether or not he has purported to do so) of giving a valid consent to the taking of a specimen of blood; and

    (d) it appears to that constable that that person's incapacity is attributable to medical reasons.

(2) A request under this section—

    (a) shall not be made to a medical practitioner who for the time being has any responsibility (apart from the request) for the clinical care of the person concerned; and

    (b) shall not be made to a medical practitioner other than a police medical practitioner unless—

        (i) it is not reasonably practicable for the request to made to a police medical practitioner; or

       (ii) it is not reasonably practicable for such a medical practitioner (assuming him to be willing to do so) to take the specimen.

(3) It shall be lawful for a medical practitioner to whom a request is made under this section, if he thinks fit—

    (a) to take a specimen of blood from the person concerned irrespective of whether that person consents; and

    (b) to provide the sample to a constable.

(4) If a specimen is taken in pursuance of a request under this section, the specimen shall not be subjected to a laboratory test unless the person from whom it was taken—

    (a) has been informed that it was taken; and

    (b) has been required by a constable to give his permission for a laboratory test of the specimen; and

    (c) has given his permission.

(5) A constable must, on requiring a person to give his permission for the purposes of this section for a laboratory test of a specimen, warn that person that a failure to give the permission may render him liable to prosecution.

(6) A person who, without reasonable excuse, fails to give his permission for a laboratory test of a specimen of blood taken from him under this section is guilty of an offence.

(7) In this section "police medical practitioner" means a medical practitioner who is engaged under any agreement to provide medical services for purposes connected with the activities of a police force.

The offence under s.7(A)(6) is only committed if the refusal to give permission is "without reasonable excuse". There is an evidential burden on the defendant, but once raised in issue, the prosecution must prove beyond reasonable doubt that there is no reasonable excuse. In the case of a specimen already obtained and available to be analysed, it is difficult to see what could be raised that the courts are likely to treat as being capable of amounting to a reasonable excuse.

Further provisions in relation to the admissibility and use of specimens in proceedings

There are further important provisions contained in s.15 and s.16 of the Road Traffic Offenders Act which set out the use which may be made of specimens, including important statutory assumptions.

The Road Traffic Offenders Act 1988 s.15:

15 Use of Specimens in Proceedings for an Offence under Sections 4 or 5 of the Road Traffic Act

(1) This section and section 16 of this Act apply in respect of proceedings for an offence under section 3A, 4 or 5 of the Road Traffic Act 1988 (driving offences connected with drink or drugs); and expressions used in this section and section 16 of this Act have the same meaning as in sections 3A to 10 of that Act.

(2) Evidence of the proportion of alcohol or any drug in a specimen of breath, blood or urine provided by or taken from the accused shall, in all cases (including cases where the specimen was not provided or taken in connection with the alleged offence), be taken into account and, subject to subsection (3) below, it shall be assumed that the proportion of alcohol in the accused's breath, blood or urine at the time of the alleged offence was not less than in the specimen.

(3) That assumption shall not be made if the accused proves—

(a) that he consumed alcohol before he provided the specimen or had it taken from him and—

(i) in relation to an offence under section 3A, after the time of the alleged offence, and

(ii) otherwise, after he had ceased to drive, attempt to drive or be in charge of a vehicle on a road or other public place, and

(b) that had he not done so the proportion of alcohol in his breath, blood or urine would not have exceeded the prescribed limit and, if it is alleged that he was unfit to drive through drink, would not have been such as to impair his ability to drive properly.

(4) A specimen of blood shall be disregarded unless—

(a) it was taken from the accused with his consent and either—

(i) in a police station by a medical practitioner or a registered health care professional; or

(ii) elsewhere by a medical practitioner; or

(b) it was taken from the accused by a medical practitioner under
section 7A of the Road Traffic Act 1988 and the accused subsequently gave his permission for a laboratory test of the specimen.

(5) Where, at the time a specimen of blood or urine was provided by the
accused, he asked to be provided with such a specimen, evidence of the
proportion of alcohol or any drug found in the specimen is not
admissible on behalf of the prosecution unless—

(a) the specimen in which the alcohol or drug was found is one of two
parts into which the specimen provided by the accused was divided
at the time it was provided, and

(b) the other part was supplied to the accused.

(5A) Where a specimen of blood was taken from the accused under section
7A of the Road Traffic Act 1988, evidence of the proportion of alcohol
or any drug found in the specimen is not admissible on behalf of the
prosecution unless—

(a) the specimen in which the alcohol or drug was found is one of two
parts into which the specimen taken from the accused was divided
at the time it was taken; and

(b) any request to be supplied with the other part which was made by
the accused at the time when he gave his permission for a
laboratory test of the specimen was complied with.

The Road Traffic Act 1988 s.16:

16   Documentary Evidence as to Specimens in such Proceedings

(1) Evidence of the proportion of alcohol or a drug in a specimen of breath,
blood or urine may, subject to subsections (3) and (4) below and to
section 15(5) and (5A) of this Act, be given by the production of a
document or documents purporting to be whichever of the following is
appropriate, that is to say—

(a) a statement automatically produced by the device by which the
proportion of alcohol in a specimen of breath was measured and a
certificate signed by a constable (which may but need not be
contained in the same document as the statement) that the
statement relates to a specimen provided by the accused at the
date and time shown in the statement, and

(b) a certificate signed by an authorised analyst as to the proportion of
alcohol or any drug found in a specimen of blood or urine
identified in the certificate.

(2) Subject to subsections (3) and (4) below, evidence that a specimen of
blood was taken from the accused with his consent by a medical

practitioner or a registered health care professional may be given by the production of a document purporting to certify that fact and to be signed by a medical practitioner or a registered health care professional.

(3) Subject to subsection (4) below—

   (a) a document purporting to be such a statement or such a certificate (or both such a statement and such a certificate) as is mentioned in subsection (1)(a) above is admissible in evidence on behalf of the prosecution in pursuance of this section only if a copy of it either has been handed to the accused when the document was produced or has been served on him not later than seven days before the hearing, and

   (b) any other document is so admissible only if a copy of it has been served on the accused not later than seven days before the hearing.

(4) A document purporting to be a certificate (or so much of a document as purports to be a certificate) is not so admissible if the accused, not later than three days before the hearing or within such further time as the court may in special circumstances allow, has served notice on the prosecutor requiring the attendance at the hearing of the person by whom the document purports to be signed.

(5) (6) . . .

(7) In this section "authorised analyst" means—

   (a) any person possessing the qualifications prescribed by regulations made under section 27 of the Food Safety Act 1990 as qualifying persons for appointment as public analysts under those Acts, and

   (b) any other person authorised by the Secretary of State to make analyses for the purposes of this section.

Sections 15 and 16 of the Road Traffic Offenders Act 1988 make admissible the results of the analysis of a specimen lawfully required under s.7 of the Road Traffic Act 1988. Section 15(2) specifically requires that such evidence be taken into account.

Where, under s.8, the defendant has requested that a breath specimen be replaced with an alternative specimen of blood or urine, the prosecutor may not subsequently rely on the breath reading to prove an offence where the defendant provides the alternative specimen.[59] However, s.8(2) does not render evidence of the breath specimen inadmissible for all purposes. Provided that the prosecution is based on the result of a blood or urine analysis, the results of the breath test may still be given in evidence if there is a relevant and clearly identified purpose for so doing, such as to establish the correct procedure was followed,[60] or to counter a submission of unreliability in relation to the blood analysis.[61]

---

[59] Road Traffic Act 1988 s.8(2).
[60] *Yhnell v DPP* (1988) 153 J.P. 364; [1989] R.T.R. 250.
[61] *Slasor v DPP* [1999] R.T.R. 432.

Section 15(2) creates a statutory assumption that the proportion of alcohol in the accused's breath, blood or urine at the time of the alleged offence was not less than in the specimen. This is an irrebuttable presumption in that it is not open to a defendant to lead evidence to establish otherwise, except in the circumstances set out in s.15(3). There is apparently no such bar in relation to the prosecution seeking to establish a higher reading at the time of driving where a considerable period had elapsed between the driving and the provision of the sample.[62]

Under s.15(3) the statutory assumption will not apply if the defendant proves that he consumed alcohol after the time of the alleged offence but before he provided the specimen and that had he not done so the proportion of alcohol in his breath, blood or urine would not have exceeded the prescribed limit or would not have been such as to impair his ability to drive properly.

Usually such proof will require expert evidence by way of a back calculation. As the burden of proof is on the defendant, and is a full legal rather than evidential burden, the required standard of proof is the balance of probabilities.

Back calculations

The principle of a back calculation is to establish the alcohol level at an earlier point in time than the time when the specimen is taken. However, it is an imprecise calculation as the rate at which alcohol is eliminated from the body varies between individuals, is not a steady rate, and an alcohol level will continue to rise for some time after ingestion of alcohol, the rate of absorption of alcohol from the stomach also being a variable.

Requirement to serve documentary evidence

The requirement as to service in s.16 of the Road Traffic Offenders Act 1988 of documentary evidence applies only where the print-out or certificate is relied upon to establish that the proportion of alcohol in the sample is in excess of the prescribed limit. It is not the only method of proof, and evidence of the read-out of a breathalyser machine can be given by a police officer administering the test who observed the digital reading at the time, where for some reason the print-out is no longer available. However, to be admissible, the officer must also give evidence of the self-calibration of the device to establish reliability. It is not necessary to establish specific evidence of the purging process; evidence of due calibration was sufficient in the absence of any evidence of malfunction.[63] A certificate as to the blood analysis can only be admitted under s.16(1)(b) if signed by an "authorised" analyst.[64] However, an expert may give oral evidence, or evidence may be admitted in the form of a statement under s.9 of the Criminal Justice Act 1967, of the proportion of alcohol analysed in the blood

---

[62] *Gumbley v Cunningham* [1989] R.T.R. 49. Note that the prosecution will have to establish that the amount of alcohol would have exceeded the permitted limit, beyond reasonable doubt.

[63] *DPP v Parkin* [1989] Crim. L.R. 379.

[64] Road Traffic Act 1988 s.16(7).

sample. Where the evidence is admissible in this form, and is not adduced as a certificate under s.16(1)(b), there is no requirement for the analyst to be "authorised".[65]

Where it is sought to rely on a certificate for some other reason, for example to show the machine was not reliable and therefore pursuant to s.7(3)(b) or (bb) the requirement for an alternative specimen under s.7(4) was lawful, that document need not have been served prior to the hearing.[66]

---

[65] *R (on the application of CPS) v Sedgemoor Justices* [2007] EWHC 1803 (Admin). However, those who sought to rely on the evidence of a skilled but unauthorised analyst needed to be in a position to demonstrate the necessary expertise in handling the technique involved. In every case the court had to be satisfied that the evidence being tendered was expert and reliable. Providing it was, that evidence was admissible whether it was tendered by way of a certificate from an authorised analyst or by the evidence of a demonstrated expert.

[66] *Jubb v DPP* [2002] EWHC 2317.

Fail to provide specimen for analysis (drive/attempt to drive)	Road Traffic Act 1988, s.7(6)

Triable only summarily:
Maximum penalty: Level 5 fine and/or 6 months

- Must endorse and disqualify for at least 12 months
- Must disqualify for **at least** 2 years if offender has had two or more disqualifications for periods of 56 days or more in preceding 3 years – **refer to page 159 and consult your legal adviser for further guidance**
- Must disqualify for **at least** 3 years if offender has been convicted of a relevant offence in preceding 10 years – **refer to page 159 and consult your legal adviser for further guidance**.

If there is a delay in sentencing after conviction, consider interim disqualification

Note: the final column below provides guidance regarding the length of disqualification that may be appropriate in cases to which the 3 year minimum applies. The period to be imposed in any individual case will depend on an assessment of all the relevant circumstances, including the length of time since the earlier ban was imposed and the gravity of the current offence.

OFFENCE SERIOUSNESS (CULPABILITY AND HARM)
A. IDENTIFY THE APPROPRIATE STARTING POINT
Starting points based on first time offender pleading not guilty

Examples of nature of activity	Starting point	Range	Disqualification	Disqual. 2nd offence in 10 years
Defendant refused test when had honestly held but unreasonable excuse	Band C fine	Band C fine	12 – 16 months	36 – 40 months
Deliberate refusal or deliberate failure	Low level community order	Band C fine to high level community order	17 – 28 months	36 – 52 months
Deliberate refusal or deliberate failure where evidence of serious impairment	12 weeks custody	High level community order to 26 weeks custody	29 – 36 months	36 – 60 months

OFFENCE SERIOUSNESS (CULPABILITY AND HARM)
B. CONSIDER THE EFFECT OF AGGRAVATING AND MITIGATING FACTORS
(OTHER THAN THOSE WITHIN EXAMPLES ABOVE)
Common aggravating and mitigating factors are identified in the pullout card. The following may be particularly relevant but these lists are not exhaustive:

Factors indicating higher culpability	Factors indicating lower culpability
1. Evidence of unacceptable standard of driving 2. LGV, HGV, PSV etc. 3. Obvious state of intoxication 4. Driving for hire or reward Factor indicating greater degree of harm 1. Involved in accident	1. Genuine but unsuccessful attempt to provide specimen

FORM A PRELIMINARY VIEW OF THE APPROPRIATE SENTENCE, THEN CONSIDER OFFENDER MITIGATION
Common factors are identified in the pullout card

CONSIDER A REDUCTION FOR GUILTY PLEA

CONSIDER OFFERING DRINK/DRIVE REHABILITATION COURSE

CONSIDER ANCILLARY ORDERS
Refer to pages 142-148 for guidance on available ancillary orders

DECIDE SENTENCE

GIVE REASONS

© The Sentencing Guidelines Council

Road Traffic Act 1988, s.7(6)	**Fail to provide specimen for analysis (in charge)**

Triable only summarily:
Maximum penalty: Level 4 fine and/or 3 months

Must endorse and may disqualify. If no disqualification, impose 10 points.

OFFENCE SERIOUSNESS (CULPABILITY AND HARM)
A. IDENTIFY THE APPROPRIATE STARTING POINT
Starting points based on first time offender pleading not guilty

Examples of nature of activity	Starting point	Range
Defendant refused test when had honestly held but unreasonable excuse	Band B fine	Band B fine 10 points
Deliberate refusal or deliberate failure	Band C fine	Band C fine to medium level community order Consider disqualification OR 10 points
Deliberate refusal or deliberate failure where evidence of serious impairment	Medium level community order	Low level community order to 6 weeks custody Disqualify 6 -12 months

OFFENCE SERIOUSNESS (CULPABILITY AND HARM)
B. CONSIDER THE EFFECT OF AGGRAVATING AND MITIGATING FACTORS
(OTHER THAN THOSE WITHIN EXAMPLES ABOVE)
Common aggravating and mitigating factors are identified in the pullout card. The following may be particularly relevant but these lists are not exhaustive:

Factors indicating higher culpability	Factors indicating lower culpability
1. Obvious state of intoxication 2. LGV, HGV, PSV etc. 3. High likelihood of driving 4. Driving for hire or reward	1. Genuine but unsuccessful attempt to provide specimen 2. Low likelihood of driving

FORM A PRELIMINARY VIEW OF THE APPROPRIATE SENTENCE, THEN CONSIDER OFFENDER MITIGATION
Common factors are identified in the pullout card

CONSIDER A REDUCTION FOR GUILTY PLEA

CONSIDER ANCILLARY ORDERS
Refer to pages 142-148 for guidance on available ancillary orders

DECIDE SENTENCE

GIVE REASONS

Endorsement, Requirement to

(Reference: Wilkinson's Road Traffic Offences, Ch.19.)

Every endorsable offence carries fixed or variable penalty points that must be ordered to be endorsed on an offender's licence, together with details of the offence including the date when the offence was committed.[1] If the court orders a disqualification, particulars of that disqualification must be endorsed on the licence. The requirement to order endorsement does not arise until the point of sentence, and so no endorsement can be ordered by the court when adjourning for a report, deferring sentence, remitting to another court or committing to the Crown Court.[2]

The Road Traffic Act 1988 s.44 sets out the requirement to order endorsement of driving licences.

44   ENDORSEMENT OF LICENCES

(1) Where a person is convicted of an offence involving obligatory endorsement, the court must order there to be endorsed on the counterpart of any licence held by him particulars of the conviction and also—

   (a) if the court orders him to be disqualified, particulars of the disqualification, or

   (b) if the court does not order him to be disqualified—

      (i) particulars of the offence, including the date when it was committed, and

      (ii) the penalty points to be attributed to the offence.

(2) Where the court does not order the person convicted to be disqualified, it need not make an order under subsection (1) above if for special reasons it thinks fit not to do so.

(3) . . .

(4) This section is subject to section 48 of this Act.

"Any" licence issued to a driver under Pt III of the Road Traffic Act is required to be endorsed. Other licences, e.g. international permits or foreign licences, cannot be endorsed. Even if the driver does not actually have a licence, the order for endorsement will still be made and a driver record created and kept by the Driver Vehicle Licensing Agency.

---

[1] CPR 2005 r.55.1 also requires particulars of the sentence to be included.
[2] In such circumstances the court does have power to order an interim disqualification—see Orders for interim disqualification.

Penalty points, requirement to attribute to an offence

Where there is a requirement to endorse, the number of penalty points to be attributed to the offence is as set out in s.28 and Sch.2 to the Road Traffic Act 1988.

28 PENALTY POINTS TO BE ATTRIBUTED TO AN OFFENCE

(1) Where a person is convicted of an offence involving obligatory endorsement, then, subject to the following provisions of this section, the number of penalty points to be attributed to the offence is—

    (a) the number shown in relation to the offence in the last column of Part I or Part II of Schedule 2 to this Act, or

    (b) where a range of numbers is shown, a number within that range.

(2) Where a person is convicted of an offence committed by aiding, abetting, counseling or procuring, or inciting to the commission of, an offence involving obligatory disqualification, then, subject to the following provisions of this section, the number of penalty points to be attributed to the offence is ten.

(3) Where both a range of numbers and a number followed by the words "(fixed penalty)" is shown in the last column of Part I of Schedule 2 to this Act in relation to an offence, that number is the number of penalty points to be attributed to the offence for the purposes of sections 57(5) and 77(5) of this Act; and, where only a range of numbers is shown there, the lowest number in the range is the number of penalty points to be attributed to the offence for those purposes.

(4) Where a person is convicted (whether on the same occasion or not) of two or more offences committed on the same occasion and involving obligatory endorsement, the total number of penalty points to be attributed to them is the number or highest number that would be attributed on a conviction of one of them (so that if the convictions are on different occasions the number of penalty points to be attributed to the offences on the later occasion or occasions shall be restricted accordingly).

(5) In a case where (apart from this subsection) subsection (4) above would apply to two or more offences, the court may if it thinks fit determine that that subsection shall not apply to the offences (or, where three or more offences are concerned, to any one or more of them).

(6) Where a court makes such a determination it shall state its reasons in open court and, if it is a magistrates' court, or in Scotland a court of summary jurisdiction, shall cause them to be entered in the register (in Scotland, record) of its proceedings.

Where the Schedule sets a range of variable points, it will be for the court to determine how many should be endorsed for that offence, taking into account the relative seriousness of the offending. Where an offender is convicted of more than one offence carrying penalty points, the offences having been committed on the same occasion, s.28(4) provides that the maximum number of points to be imposed is limited to that applicable to highest number that could be imposed for any one of them. However, s.28(5) allows a court to disapply subs.(4), and where it does so, reasons must be given in open court and entered on the register.

Where an offender is convicted of one or more offences, and the court makes an order for disqualification under s.34, no further penalty points are to be endorsed for any other offences of which he had been convicted on that occasion.[3]

---

[3] s.44(1), considered in *Martin v DPP* [2000] R.T.R. 188.

Effect of endorsement

Endorsement is an important order, as previous endorsements may count as qualifying for the purpose of obligatory penalty points disqualification under s.35 of the Road Traffic Offenders Act 1988. For this reason an order for endorsement carries with it a requirement that the details remain endorsed on the licence for the prescribed periods set out in the Road Traffic Act 1988 s.45.

45   EFFECT OF ENDORSEMENT

(1) An order that any particulars or penalty points are to be endorsed on the counterpart of any licence held by the person convicted shall, whether he is at the time the holder of a licence or not, operate as an order that the counterpart of any licence he may then hold or may subsequently obtain is to be so endorsed until he becomes entitled under subsection (4) below to have a licence issued to him with its counterpart free from the particulars or penalty points.

(2) On the issue of a new licence to a person, any particulars or penalty points ordered to be endorsed on the counterpart of any licence held by him shall be entered on the counterpart of the licence unless he has become entitled under subsection (4) below to have a licence issued to him with its counterpart free from those particulars or penalty points.

(3) . . .

(4) A person the counterpart of whose licence has been ordered to be endorsed is entitled to have issued to him with effect from the end of the period for which the endorsement remains effective a new licence with a counterpart free from the endorsement if, he applies for a new licence in pursuance of section 97(1) of the Road Traffic Act 1988, surrenders any subsisting licence and its counterpart, pays the fee prescribed by regulations under Part III of that Act and satisfies the other requirements of section 97(1).

(5) An endorsement ordered on a person's conviction of an offence remains effective (subject to subsections (6) and (7) below)—

   (a) if an order is made for the disqualification of the offender, until four years have elapsed since the conviction, and
   (b) if no such order is made, until either—

      (i) four years have elapsed since the commission of the offence, or
      (ii) an order is made for the disqualification of the offender under section 35 of this Act.

(6) Where the offence was one under section 1 or 2 of that Act (causing death by dangerous driving and dangerous driving), the endorsement

remains in any case effective until four years have elapsed since the conviction.

(7) Where the offence was one—

(a) section 3A, 4(1) or 5(1)(a) of that Act (driving offences connected with drink or drugs), or

(b) under section 7(6) of that Act (failing to provide specimen) involving obligatory disqualification,

the endorsement remains effective until eleven years have elapsed since the conviction.

The Act requires that endorsements must remain on the licence for:

a) four years from the date of the offence if no order for disqualification was made (unless an order is subsequently made disqualifying the driver under s.35 of the Act, when all previously endorsed penalty points are thereby removed from the licence);

b) four years from the date of conviction if an order for disqualification was made, or the offence is one of causing death by dangerous driving or dangerous driving;

c) 11 years for offences involving drink or drugs, under ss.3A, 4(1) or 5(1)(a) and 7(6) of the Road Traffic Act.

Since the order to endorse is obligatory in the absence of special reasons not to, an omission to make the order can be corrected under s.142(1) of the Magistrates' Courts Act 1980, which gives a court power to re-open a case to rectify a mistake.

If a court decides not to order obligatory endorsement or obligatory disqualification having found special reasons for not doing so (see **Special reasons not to disqualify/endorse**), it must give reasons for that decision in open court and those reasons must be recorded in the court register.

Endorsable Offence Codes

The information in the codes set out below is derived from the publication *DVLA Court Guidelines on Driver Notifications*, issued by the Driver and Vehicle Licensing Agency, Swansea (A671), as amended.

DVLA Endorsement Codes

Code	Offence	Penalty points
	Accident offences	
AC10	Failing to stop after an accident	5–10
AC20	Failing to give particulars or to report an accident within 24 hours	5–10
AC30	Undefined accident offences	4–9
	Disqualified driver	
BA10	Driving while disqualified by order of court	6
BA30	Attempting to drive while disqualified by order of court	6
	Careless driving	
CD10	Driving without due care and attention	3–9
CD20	Driving without reasonable consideration for other road users	3–9
CD30	Driving without due care and attention or without reasonable consideration for other road users	3–9
CD40	Causing death by careless driving when unfit through drink	3–11
CD50	Causing death by careless driving when unfit through drugs	3–11
CD60	Causing death by careless driving with alcohol level above the limit	3–11
CD70	Causing death by careless driving then failing to supply specimen for analysis	3–11
	Construction and use offences	
CU10	Using a vehicle with defective brakes	3
CU20	Causing or likely to cause danger by reason of use of unsuitable vehicle or using a vehicle with parts or accessories (excluding brakes, steering or tyres) in a dangerous condition	3
CU30	Using a vehicle with defective tyre(s)	3

Code	Offence	Penalty points
CU40	Using a vehicle with defective steering	3
CU50	Causing or likely to cause danger by reason of load or passengers	3
CU40	Using a vehicle with defective steering	3
CU50	Causing or likely to cause danger by reason of load or passengers	3
CU80	Breach of requirements as to control of vehicle, mobile telephones, etc.	3

Reckless/Dangerous driving

DD40	Dangerous driving	3–11
DD60	Manslaughter or culpable homicide while driving a motor vehicle	3–11
DD80	Causing death by dangerous driving	3–11

Drink or drugs

DR10	Driving or attempting to drive with alcohol concentration above limit	3–11
DR20	Driving or attempting to drive when unfit through drink	3–11
DR30	Driving or attempting to drive then failing to provide a specimen for analysis	3–11
DR40	In charge of a vehicle while alcohol level above limit	10
DR50	In charge of a vehicle while unfit through drink	10
DR60	Failure to provide a specimen for analysis in circumstances other than driving or attempting to drive	10
DR70	Failing to provide a specimen for breath test	4
DR80	Driving or attempting to drive when unfit through drugs	3–11
DR90	In charge of a vehicle when unfit through drugs	10

Insurance offences

IN10	Using a vehicle uninsured against third party risks	6–8

Licence offences

LC20	Driving otherwise than in accordance with a licence	3–6
LC30	Driving after making a false declaration about fitness when applying for a licence	3–6
LC40	Driving a vehicle having failed to notify a disability	3–6
LC50	Driving after a licence has been revoked or refused on medical grounds	3–6

Miscellaneous offences

MS10	Leaving a vehicle in a dangerous position	3

Code	Offence	Penalty points
MS20	Unlawful pillion riding	3
MS30	Play street offences	2
MS50	Motor racing on the highway	3–11
MS60	Offences not covered by other codes	As appropriate
MS70	Driving with uncorrected defective eyesight	3
MC80	Refusing to submit to an eyesight test	3
MS90	Failure to give information as to identity of driver, etc.	3

Motorway offences

MW10	Contravention of Special Roads Regulations (excluding speed limits)	3

Pedestrian crossings

PC10	Undefined contravention of Pedestrian Crossing Regulations	3
PC20	Contravention of Pedestrian Crossing Regulations with moving vehicle	3
PC30	Contravention of Pedestrian Crossing Regulations with stationary vehicle	3

Speed limit

SP10	Exceeding goods vehicle speed limits	3–6
SP20	Exceeding speed limit for type of vehicle (excluding goods or passenger vehicles)	3–6
SP30	Exceeding statutory speed limit on a public road	3–6
SP40	Exceeding passenger vehicle speed limit	3–6
SP50	Exceeding speed limit on a motorway	3–6
SP60	Undefined speed limit offence	3–6

Traffic Directions and signs

TS10	Failing to comply with traffic light signals	3
TS20	Failing to comply with a double white lines	3
TS30	Failing to comply with a "Stop" sign	3
TS40	Failing to comply with direction of a constable/warden	3
TS50	Failing to comply with a traffic sign (excluding stop signs, traffic lights or double white lines)	3
TS60	Failure to comply with a school crossing patrol sign	3
TS70	Undefined failure to comply with a traffic direction sign	3

Totting disqualifications

TT99	Totting-up disqualification (12 penalty points within three years)	

Code	Offence	Penalty points

Theft or unauthorised taking

UT50   Aggravated taking of a vehicle   3–11

Aiding, abetting, counselling or procuring
Offences as codes above, but with 0 changed to 2,
e.g. IN10 becomes IN12.

Causing or permitting
Offences as coded above, but 0 is changed to 4, e.g.
IN10 becomes IN14.

Inciting
Offences as coded above but 0 is changed to 6, e.g.
IN10 becomes IN16.

Miscellaneous

NE96   Disqualification for non-payment of child support

NE98   Disqualification for any offence under s.146 of the
        Powers of Criminal Courts (Sentencing) Act 2000

NE99   Non-endorsable disqualification code. To be used
        where disqualification still relevant but endorsement
        no longer applicable.

Sentence Code

In the case of sentences other than fines or disqualification, the nature of the sentence is indicated on the driving licence by the following code which provides the first character of the endorsement:

A	Imprisonment
B	Detention in a place specified by the Secretary of State
C	Suspended sentence of imprisonment
D	Suspended sentence supervision order
E	Conditional discharge
F	Bound over
G	Probation
H	Supervision order
I	No separate penalty
J	Absolute discharge
K	Attendance center
L	Detention centre (Scottish courts only)
M	Community service order
N	Cumulative sentence (Scottish courts only)
P	Youth custody sentence (Scotland): Young offender institution (England and Wales)

Q	Parent or guardian order
R	Borstal
S	Compensation order
T	Hospital or guardianship order
U	Admonition (Scottish courts only)
V	Young offender institution (Scottish courts only)
W	Care order
*	Curfew order
#	Combination order
X	Total period of partially suspended prison sentence i.e. period sentence served + period sentence suspended

If the first character of the endorsement is A, B, C, D, E, F, G, H, K, L, P, R, U, V or X, two digits and a character follow the initial character, indicating the duration of the sentence in hours, days, weeks, months or years (i.e. H, D, W, M or Y, respectively). For example, 18 months' imprisonment would be indicated by the code A 18 M. If no period is specified, the initial character is followed by three zeros.

If the first character of the endorsement is H, I, J, N, Q, S, T or W, three zeros follow the initial character. For example, absolute discharge would be indicated by the code J 000.

If the first character of the endorsement is M (community service order), three digits follow the initial character, indicating the number of hours' service (the letter H is not used). For example, 40 hours' community service would be indicated by the code M 040, 240 hours' by M 240.

If the first character of the endorsement is C (suspended prison sentence), two digits and a character follow the initial character, indicating the period the prison sentence has been suspended. For example, one month's prison suspended for one year would be indicated by A 01 M followed by C 01Y.

If the first character of the endorsement is X (partially suspended prison sentence), the code is similar. Two digits and a character follow the initial character, indicating the period of prison sentence actually served. For example, four months' imprisonment with one month to be served would be indicated by A 04M, followed by X 01 M.

Evidence

(Reference: Wilkinson's Road Traffic Offences, Ch.3.)

Road traffic offences are criminal offences and the normal rules of evidence and procedure relating to criminal trials will apply.

Any evidence put before the court must be relevant and admissible.

Evidence in relation to road traffic offences is often sought to be provided in written format. The provisions of s.9 of the Criminal Justice Act 1967 must be complied with. The contents of the statement must themselves be admissible as if the witness was testifying orally, and therefore hearsay statements will not usually be permitted.

Where matters are not in dispute, agreed admissions under s.10 of the Criminal Justice Act 1967 are a useful way to avoid wasting court time unnecessarily and assisting the court to focus on the matters that require to be determined.

Where oral evidence is to be given, s.139 of the Criminal Justice Act 2003 permits a witness to refresh his memory by reference to any document made and verified by him at an earlier time, providing that the witness states in oral evidence that the document records his recollection at that earlier time and that recollection is likely to have been significantly better at that time than it is at the time of giving oral evidence. Although it is standard practice for police witnesses to be allowed to refer to any notes made in their pocket notebooks the prosecutor must still establish the criteria under s.139; they may also be allowed to refer to any other document that meets those criteria. Care should be taken with regard to witness statements compiled from pocket notebooks to check that the police officer has signed the statement and is satisfied that the document accurately reflects his recollection. In some areas such statements are typed from the notebooks by administrative staff and the officer may not have had an opportunity to sign it, or have checked the statement against the notebook entry.

Section 139 is applicable to any witness, including the defendant. Where a witness is clearly struggling to recall events, and has previously made a witness statement, the party calling that witness should seek to allow the witness to be allowed to refresh their memory from that statement.

Expert evidence

(Reference: Wilkinson's Road Traffic Offences, Ch.3.)

The opinion of a witness is inadmissible unless he is an expert giving an opinion on matters within his expertise for which he has special knowledge and experience. This does not necessarily mean the witness must have a string of relevant qualifications; considerable experience in the field may qualify a witness to give an expert opinion.[1] An expert may give opinion evidence of the work of other experts in his field, such evidence not being excluded as hearsay.[2]

An expert witness may be permitted to be present in the courtroom while the evidence is being given.

An expert report is admissible as evidence in criminal proceedings, whether or not the person making the report attends to give oral evidence, but leave of the court will be required.[3] If leave is given, the report will stand as evidence of any fact or opinion the expert witness could have given as oral evidence. In determining whether to grant leave, the court must have regard to the following:

a) the contents of the report;

b) the reason why the expert is not to give oral evidence;

c) the risk of unfairness to the accused if the report is admitted or excluded, taking into account the ability to controvert statements in the report if the witness does not attend;

d) any other relevant circumstances.

Part 24 of the CPR 2005 imposes a requirement on the parties to criminal proceedings to disclose expert evidence. If any party proposes to adduce expert evidence of fact or opinion (otherwise than in relation to sentence) he must furnish the other party with a statement in writing of such evidence proposed to be adduced, as soon as practicable.[4] A party may request a copy of, or access to records of any observations, test or calculation or other procedure on which the

---

[1] e.g. an experienced police officer is likely to be expert in determining whether a person is "drunk", and may therefore express such an opinion. See *R (on the application of Doughty) v Ely Magistrates' Court* [2008] EWHC 522 (Admin) where magistrates should have considered the qualifications and experience of the witness in determining whether he could give his expert opinion in evidence, and not taken into account whether he had recent knowledge equivalent to that of an expert called by the prosecution.

[2] *R. v Abadom* [1983] 1 All E.R. 364.

[3] Criminal Justice Act 1988 s.30.

[4] CPR 2005 r.24.1. See also the standard directions which operate as default directions contained in the case progression forms for use in magistrates' courts in accordance with the Consolidated Criminal Practice Direction.

expert findings are based. If r.24.1 is not complied with, such evidence cannot be adduced in the proceedings without leave of the court.[5]

Application of local and specialised knowledge

Local and specialised knowledge is likely to arise in proceedings relating to road traffic offences. The use of local knowledge is implicit in the concept of local magistrates and local justice, and such knowledge could not and should not be excluded from the court's mind.[6] However, magistrates should be "extremely circumspect" when using local knowledge. The court should make known to prosecution and defence that local knowledge is being relied upon and afford advocates the opportunity to comment.[7]

A magistrate with specialist knowledge is entitled to use that knowledge in interpreting or assessing the evidence already before the court and communicate his views to his fellow justices, provided he does not give evidence contradicting the evidence given in court.[8] Again, fairness would suggest that such specialist knowledge be made known to the parties so that they may be given an opportunity to comment.

---

[5] The standard directions that automatically apply in magistrates' courts when a plea of not guilty is entered provide for the disclosure of expert's reports. Courts are increasingly taking a robust approach if such directions are not complied with for no good reason and late applications are made to the court. The most recent amendments to the CPR in Pt 3 clarify the power to impose sanctions for non-compliance.

[6] *Chesson v Jordan* [1981] Crim. L.R. 333.

[7] *Bowman v DPP* (1990) 154 J.P. 524.

[8] *Wetherall v Harrison* [1976] R.T.R. 125.

Failure to give details

(Reference: Wilkinson's Road Traffic Offences, Ch.7.)

The duty to give information arises under separate sections of the relevant legislation. A person who refuses to provide such information may be guilty of a specific offence under the relevant legislation, but will not be guilty of an offence of obstructing the police unless he deliberately gives false information.[1]

Section 170 of the Road Traffic Act 1988 imposes duties to stop and provide information following an accident. A failure to do so may amount to an offence (see **Accident, Duty of driver to stop, report accident and give information or show document**).

Section 172 of the Road Traffic Act 1988 imposes a duty to give information as to the driver of a motor vehicle. A failure to provide such information is an offence (see **Identity of driver, Failure to give information as to**).

There are other instances where information may be required of owners and drivers.

Section 171 of the Road Traffic Act provides as follows:

171 DUTY OF OWNER OF MOTOR VEHICLE TO GIVE INFORMATION FOR VERIFYING COMPLIANCE WITH REQUIREMENT OF COMPULSORY INSURANCE OR SECURITY

(1) For the purpose of determining whether a motor vehicle was or was not being driven in contravention of section 143 of this Act on any occasion when the driver was required under section 165(1) or 170 of this Act to produce such a certificate of insurance or security, or other evidence, as is mentioned in section 165(2)(a) of this Act, the owner of the vehicle must give such information as he may be required, by or on behalf of a chief officer of police, to give.

(2) A person who fails to comply with the requirement of subsection (1) above is guilty of an offence.

(3) In this section "owner", in relation to a vehicle which is the subject of a hiring agreement, includes each party to the agreement.

The owner of a motor vehicle must give such information as may be required by or on behalf of a chief officer of police for the purpose of determining whether an offence has been committed in relation to a vehicle being used without insurance, on any occasion when the driver was required to produce a certificate of insurance.

---

[1] *R. v Field* [1964] 3 All E.R. 269.

The Road Traffic Act 1988 s.168:

168 Failure to Give, or Giving False, Name and Address in Case of Reckless or Careless or Inconsiderate Driving or Cycling

Any of the following persons—

(a) the driver of a mechanically propelled vehicle who is alleged to have committed an offence under section 2 or 3 of this Act, or

(b) the rider of a cycle who is alleged to have committed an offence under section 28 or 29 of this Act, who refuses, on being so required by any person having reasonable ground for so requiring, to give his name or address, or gives a false name or address, is guilty of an offence.

Section 168 imposes on a driver of a mechanically propelled vehicle where he is alleged to have driven carelessly or recklessly a duty to give his details to any person having reasonable grounds for requiring them. The information provided must be correct; giving false details amounts to an offence. It will be for the court to determine whether any person had reasonable grounds for making such a request. The fact that the defendant did not think such reasonable grounds existed will not be a defence where the court finds otherwise on the facts.

Offence	Mode of trial	Section	Imprisonment	Fine	Disqualification	Penalty Points	Endorsement code
Failing to give certain names and addresses or produce certain documents	Summary	165	No	Level 3	—	—	—
Refusing to give, or giving false name and address in case of reckless, careless or inconsiderate driving	Summary	168	No	Level 3	—	—	—
Failure by owner to give police information regarding insurance	Summary	171	No	Level 4	—	—	—

Forgery of documents

(Reference: Wilkinson's Road Traffic Offences, Ch.16.)

Sections 173 and 174 of the Road Traffic Act 1988 create offences where a person:

a) with intent to deceive forges, or alters or uses or lends or allows the use of a document of thing or makes or has in his possession a document so closely resembling a certificate as to be calculated to deceive; or

b) makes a false statement or withholds any material information for the purpose of obtaining such a certificate.

Section 173 creates the offences in respect of false documents.

173 FORGERY OF DOCUMENTS, ETC.

(1) A person who, with intent to deceive—

    (a) forges, alters or uses a document or other thing to which this section applies, or

    (b) lends to, or allows to be used by, any other person a document or other thing to which this section applies, or

    (c) makes or has in his possession any document or other thing so closely resembling a document or other thing to which this section applies as to be calculated to deceive, is guilty of an offence.

(2) This section applies to the following documents and other things—

    (a) any licence under any Part of this Act or, in the case of a licence to drive, any counterpart of such a licence,

    (aa) any counterpart of a Northern Ireland licence or Community licence,

    (b) any test certificate, goods vehicle test certificate, plating certificate, certificate of conformity or Minister's approval certificate (within the meaning of Part II of this Act),

    (c) any certificate required as a condition of any exception prescribed under section 14 of this Act,

    (cc) any seal required by regulations made under section 41 of this Act with respect to speed limiters,

    (d) any plate containing particulars required to be marked on a vehicle by regulations under section 41 of this Act or containing other particulars required to be marked on a goods vehicle by sections 54 to 58 of this Act or regulations under those sections,

    (dd) any document evidencing the appointment of an examiner under section 66A of this Act,

(e) any records required to be kept by virtue of section 74 of this Act,

(f) any document which, in pursuance of section 89(3) . . . of this Act, is issued as evidence of the result of a test of competence to drive,

(ff) any certificate provided for by regulations under section 97(3A) of this Act relating to the completion of a training course for motor cyclists,

(g) any certificate under section 133A or any badge or certificate prescribed by regulations made by virtue of section 135 of this Act,

(h) any certificate of insurance or certificate of security under Part VI of this Act,

(j) any document produced as evidence of insurance in pursuance of Regulation 6 of the Motor Vehicles (Compulsory Insurance) (No.2) Regulations 1973,

(k) any document issued under regulations made by the Secretary of State in pursuance of his power under section 165(2)(a) of this Act to prescribe evidence which may be produced in lieu of a certificate of insurance or a certificate of security, . . .

(l) any international road haulage permit, and

(m) a certificate of the kind referred to in section 34B(1) of the Road Traffic Offenders Act 1988.

(3) In the application of this section to England and Wales "forges" means makes a false document or other thing in order that it may be used as genuine.

(4) In this section "counterpart", "Community licence" and "Northern Ireland licence" have the same meanings as in Part III of this Act.

Section 174 creates the offences in relation to false statements and withholding material information.

174 FALSE STATEMENTS AND WITHHOLDING MATERIAL INFORMATION

(1) A person who knowingly makes a false statement for the purpose—

(a) of obtaining the grant of a licence under any Part of this Act to himself or any other person, or

(b) of preventing the grant of any such licence, or

(c) of procuring the imposition of a condition or limitation in relation to any such licence, or

(d) of securing the entry or retention of the name of any person in the register of approved instructors maintained under Part V of this Act, or

(dd) of obtaining the grant to any person of a certificate under section 133A of this Act, or

(e) of obtaining the grant of an international road haulage permit to himself or any other person, is guilty of an offence.

(2) A person who, in supplying information or producing documents for the purposes either of sections 53 to 60 and 63 of this Act or of regulations made under sections 49 to 51, 61, 62 and 66(3) of this Act—

    (a) makes a statement which he knows to be false in a material particular or recklessly makes a statement which is false in a material particular, or

    (b) produces, provides, sends or otherwise makes use of a document which he knows to be false in a material particular or recklessly produces, provides, sends or otherwise makes use of a document which is false in a material particular,

is guilty of an offence.

(3) A person who—

    (a) knowingly produces false evidence for the purposes of regulations under section 66(1) of this Act, or

    (b) knowingly makes a false statement in a declaration required to be made by the regulations,

is guilty of an offence.

(4) A person who—

    (a) wilfully makes a false entry in any record required to be made or kept by regulations under section 74 of this Act, or

    (b) with intent to deceive, makes use of any such entry which he knows to be false,

is guilty of an offence.

(5) A person who makes a false statement or withholds any material information for the purpose of obtaining the issue—

    (a) of a certificate of insurance or certificate of security under Part VI of this Act, or

    (b) of any document issued under regulations made by the Secretary of State in pursuance of his power under section 165(2)(a) of this Act to prescribe evidence which may be produced in lieu of a certificate of insurance or a certificate of security,

is guilty of an offence.

"Forges" means making a false document or other thing in order that it may be used as genuine.[1]

The offences under s.173 require the prosecutor to prove intention on the part of the defendant to deceive. No such requirement attaches to the offences under s.174. The offence will be committed if a statement is made, and is in fact false, regardless of whether the defendant was aware that it was false; the offence will be committed if material information is withheld (itself a conscious action) even in the absence of a dishonest motive.

The offences created by s.173 of the Act are triable either way, and so may, if appropriate and the defendant so consents, be tried in a magistrates' court. See **Procedure**.

---

[1] Road Traffic Act 1988 s.173(3).

Offence	Mode of trial	Section	Imprisonment	Fine	Disqualification	Penalty Points	Endorsement code
Forgery, etc. of licences and other documents	Either way	173	2 years on indictment 6 months summarily	Level 5	—	—	—
Making certain false statements and withholding information	Summarily	174	No	Level 4	—	—	—

Guilty plea, written notification of

(Reference: Wilkinson's Road Traffic Offences, Ch.2.)

Section 12 of the Magistrates' Courts Act permits an accused to enter a written plea of guilty to certain summary offences commenced by way of summons. Offences to which the procedure cannot be applied are those which carry imprisonment of more than three months. Many road traffic offences can be, and are, dealt with under this procedure.

The prosecutor must serve on the accused the summons, a notice containing information as to the effect of the provisions of s.12, a concise statement of the facts of the offence or a copy of written statements complying with s.9 of the Criminal Justice Act 1967, together with any information about the accused that will be given to the court if he pleads guilty (i.e. a notice of intention to cite previous convictions).[1]

The notice containing information as to the effect of the provisions of s.12 will provide for an accused to notify to the court his plea of guilty and a request that his case be dealt with in his absence.[2] The accused is also required to give his date of birth and state his sex when giving such a notification in relation to an offence carrying obligatory or discretionary disqualification.[3]

Where such a plea has been notified, the court may proceed to hear and dispose of the case in the accused's absence as if he had attended and pleaded guilty. Before accepting the written plea and convicting the accused, the court must require the clerk of the court to read out the statement of facts, or the statements served with the summons and any information about the accused, the notification of the guilty plea and any submissions received with that notification which the accused wishes to be brought to the attention of the court with a view to mitigation of sentence. No other statement relating to the facts of the offence charged or any other information relating to the accused other than that previously served is permitted to be put before the court.[4]

Where the court proceeds under s.12(5) of the Act to convict in absence, it may proceed to sentence in absence. If the court is considering any form of custodial sentence (suspended or immediate), the court cannot proceed to sentence in absence and must adjourn for the defendant to attend.[5]

Similarly, if the court is considering imposing a driving disqualification, the proceedings must be adjourned to allow the defendant to be informed and an opportunity to attend.[6] Where on the adjourned hearing, the defendant does not attend having been served with a notice stating the reason for the adjournment

---

[1] s.12(1)(b) and (3) of the Magistrates' Courts Act 1980.
[2] s.12(4) of the Magistrates' Courts Act 1980.
[3] Road Traffic Offenders Act 1988 s.8.
[4] s.12(7) and (8) of the Magistrates' Courts Act 1980.
[5] s.11(3) of the Magistrates' Courts Act 1980.
[6] s.11(4) of the Magistrates' Courts Act 1980.

and the intention to impose a disqualification, the court may proceed to sentence in absence and impose such an order for disqualification.

The court is not required to proceed with a hearing and convict the accused in absence on the basis of his written plea, and may adjourn the hearing for the accused to attend, in which case the notification of plea is ineffective.[7] This is often the case where the plea is deemed equivocal.

An accused who has given a written notification of a guilty plea may withdraw that indication in writing at any time before the hearing.[8]

A written notification of a guilty plea may be given by the accused or a legal representative acting on his behalf.[9] Notification of withdrawal of a written plea may be given by the accused or on his behalf.[10]

---

[7] s.12(9) of the Magistrates' Courts Act 1980.
[8] s.12(6) of the Magistrates' Courts Act 1980.
[9] s.12(4) of the Magistrates' Courts Act 1980.
[10] s.12(6) does not appear to require the person acting on behalf of the accused to be his legal representative.

Highway Code

The Highway Code is a code comprising directions for the guidance of persons using roads, issued under s.45 of the Road Traffic Act 1930, as revised from time to time. The code was updated in 2007 and is available in paper copy and to view on government websites.[1]

A failure on the part of a person to observe a provision of the Highway Code shall not of itself render that person liable to criminal proceedings of any kind but any such failure may in any proceedings (whether civil or criminal) be relied upon by any party to the proceedings as tending to establish or negative any liability which is in question in those proceedings.[2] In other words, a breach of the highway code is not conclusive, but may be of evidential effect. Compliance with the code does not mean that a person cannot have been careless or negligent in the circumstances.[3]

The following are useful extracts from the Code:

Speed Limits
124
You **MUST NOT** exceed the maximum speed limits for the road and for your vehicle (see the table). The presence of street lights generally means that there is a 30 mph (48 km/h) speed limit unless otherwise specified.
[Law RTRA sects 81, 86, 89 & sch 6]

125
The speed limit is the absolute maximum and does not mean it is safe to drive at that speed irrespective of conditions. Driving at speeds too fast for the road and traffic conditions is dangerous. You should always reduce your speed when

- the road layout or condition presents hazards, such as bends
- sharing the road with pedestrians, cyclists and horse riders, particularly children, and motorcyclists
- weather conditions make it safer to do so
- driving at night as it is more difficult to see other road users.

---

[1] *http://www.direct.gov.uk* [Accessed May 14, 2008].
[2] Road Traffic Act 1988 s.38(7).
[3] *Goke v Willett* [1973] R.T.R. 422.

	Built-up areas *	Single carriage-ways	Dual carriage-ways	Motorways
Type of vehicle	**mph** (km/h)	**mph** (km/h)	**mph** (km/h)	**mph** (km/h)
Cars & motorcycles (including car-derived vans up to 2 tonnes maximum laden weight)	**30** (48)	**60** (96)	**70** (112)	**70** (112)
Cars towing caravans or trailers (including car-derived vans and motorcycles)	**30** (48)	**50** (80)	**60** (96)	**60** (96)
Buses, coaches and minibuses (not exceeding 12 metres in overall length)	**30** (48)	**50** (80)	**60** (96)	**70** (112)
Goods vehicles (not exceeding 7.5 tonnes maximum laden weight)	**30** (48)	**50** (80)	**60** (96)	**70** (112) **
Goods vehicles (exceeding 7.5 tonnes maximum laden weight)	**30** (48)	**40** (64)	**50** (80)	**60** (96)

* The 30 mph limit usually applies to all traffic on all roads with street lighting unless signs show otherwise.
** 60 mph (96 km/h) if articulated or towing a trailer.

Table of Stopping distances

Drive at a speed that will allow you to stop well within the distance you can see to be clear. You should:

- leave enough space between you and the vehicle in front so that you can pull up safely if it suddenly slows down or stops. The safe rule is never to get closer than the overall stopping distance (see Typical Stopping Distances PDF below);

- allow at least a two-second gap between you and the vehicle in front on roads carrying faster-moving traffic and in tunnels where visibility is reduced. The gap should be at least doubled on wet roads and increased still further on icy roads;

- remember, large vehicles and motorcycles need a greater distance to stop. If driving a large vehicle in a tunnel, you should allow a four-second gap between you and the vehicle in front.

If you have to stop in a tunnel, leave at least a 5-metre gap between you and the vehicle in front.

Typical Stopping Distances

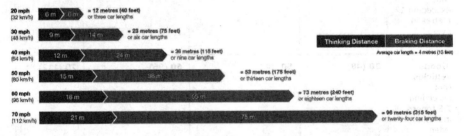

Metric Conversions

Miles	Kilometres	Miles	Kilometres
1.00	1.61	40.00	64.37
5.00	8.05	45.00	72.42
10.00	16.09	50.00	80.47
15.00	24.14	55.00	88.51
20.00	32.19	60.00	96.56
25.00	40.23	65.00	104.60
30.00	48.28	70.00	112.65
35.00	56.33		

Identity of driver, Failure to give information as to

(Reference: Wilkinson's Road Traffic Offences, Ch.7.)

The Road Traffic Act 1988 s.172 imposes a duty to give information in certain circumstances.

172 DUTY TO GIVE INFORMATION AS TO IDENTITY OF DRIVER, ETC. IN CERTAIN CIRCUMSTANCES

(1) This section applies—

    (a) to any offence under the preceding provisions of this Act except—

        (i) an offence under Part V, or

        (ii) an offence under section 13, 16, 51(2), 61(4), 67(9), 68(4), 96 or 120,

and to an offence under section 178 of this Act,

    (b) to any offence under sections 25, 26 or 27 of the Road Traffic Offenders Act 1988,

    (c) to any offence against any other enactment relating to the use of vehicles on roads, . . . and

    (d) to manslaughter, or in Scotland culpable homicide, by the driver of a motor vehicle.

(2) Where the driver of a vehicle is alleged to be guilty of an offence to which this section applies—

    (a) the person keeping the vehicle shall give such information as to the identity of the driver as he may be required to give by or on behalf of a chief officer of police, and

    (b) any other person shall if required as stated above give any information which it is in his power to give and may lead to identification of the driver.

(3) Subject to the following provisions, a person who fails to comply with a requirement under subsection (2) above shall be guilty of an offence.

(4) A person shall not be guilty of an offence by virtue of paragraph (a) of subsection (2) above if he shows that he did not know and could not with reasonable diligence have ascertained who the driver of the vehicle was.

(5) Where a body corporate is guilty of an offence under this section and the offence is proved to have been committed with the consent or connivance of, or to be attributable to neglect on the part of, a director,

manager, secretary or other similar officer of the body corporate, or a person who was purporting to act in any such capacity, he, as well as the body corporate, is guilty of that offence and liable to be proceeded against and punished accordingly.

(6) Where the alleged offender is a body corporate, or in Scotland a partnership or an unincorporated association, or the proceedings are brought against him by virtue of subsection (5) above or subsection (11) below, subsection (4) above shall not apply unless, in addition to the matters there mentioned, the alleged offender shows that no record was kept of the persons who drove the vehicle and that the failure to keep a record was reasonable.

(7) A requirement under subsection (2) may be made by written notice served by post; and where it is so made—

    (a) it shall have effect as a requirement to give the information within the period of 28 days beginning with the day on which the notice is served, and

    (b) the person on whom the notice is served shall not be guilty of an offence under this section if he shows either that he gave the information as soon as reasonably practicable after the end of that period or that it has not been reasonably practicable for him to give it.

(8) Where the person on whom a notice under subsection (7) above is to be served is a body corporate, the notice is duly served if it is served on the secretary or clerk of that body.

(9) For the purposes of section 7 of the Interpretation Act 1978 as it applies for the purposes of this section the proper address of any person in relation to the service on him of a notice under subsection (7) above is—

    (a) in the case of the secretary or clerk of a body corporate, that of the registered or principal office of that body or (if the body corporate is the registered keeper of the vehicle concerned) the registered address, and

    (b) in any other case, his last known address at the time of service.

(10) In this section—

"registered address", in relation to the registered keeper of a vehicle, means the address recorded in the record kept under the Vehicle Excise and Registration Act 1994 with respect to that vehicle as being that person's address, and

"registered keeper", in relation to a vehicle, means the person in whose name the vehicle is registered under that Act;

and references to the driver of a vehicle include references to the rider of a cycle.

Before there can be a requirement to provide information, there must be some evidence to suggest that the driver of the vehicle[1] in question has committed an offence to which the section applies. However, there is no requirement for the police to have to prove that alleged offence or give any further information about the allegation, other than to identify the vehicle, and the place and time at which it was seen.

Information can be required to be given by the registered keeper of the vehicle, or any other person. The registered keeper can be required to give such information as to the identity of the driver as may be required by or on behalf of the chief officer of police. Any other person shall give any information which it is in his power to give and may lead to the identification of the driver.[2] A constable may not seek information under this section except where authorised and acting on behalf of the chief constable.

It is not open to a person to refuse to give such information on the basis that he might incriminate himself.[3] Further, to admit in evidence answers given as a result of such a request was neither unfair nor contrary to the provisions of the European Convention on Human Rights.[4]

Attempts to argue that the requirement has been met by providing the information required orally, or by providing the written information but not signing the form, or providing the information in a separate statement or letter, have all been rejected.[5] The chief officer of police is entitled to make reasonable requirements prescribing how the person to whom the notice is addressed shall respond, and there is no need for a caution to be given before such information is required to be provided.[6] The information must also be provided within the time prescribed.

The deliberate giving of false information will also amount to an offence under the section (in addition to any other offence created) as the person will have failed to give "information which he is required to give".

Section 172(4) of the Act creates a defence for the registered keeper of the vehicle where he can show that that he did not know and could not with reasonable diligence have ascertained who the driver of the vehicle was.

Under s.172(2)(b) a person can escape conviction by showing that the required information is not in his power to give.

Where the person required to provide information denies that the vehicle in question was at the place stated at the alleged time, he may refuse to provide the information required on the basis that it is impossible to comply. In such a case, the police must then prove that the vehicle was indeed at the place at the time specified in the notice.[7]

---

[1] Not necessarily a "motor" vehicle, unless the alleged offence can only be committed by the driving of a motor vehicle.

[2] *R (on the application of Flegg) v Southampton & New Forest Justices* [2006] EWHC 396 (Admin). A s.172 notice required an accurate response and not an inaccurate or misleading statement.

[3] *Brown v Stott (Procurator Fiscal, Dunfermline)* [2001] 2 All E.R. 97.

[4] *DPP v Wilson* [2001] EWHC Admin 198; [2002] R.T.R. 6.

[5] Although see *Jones v DPP* [2004] EWHC 236 (Admin); the keeper was not required to do so entirely on the official form sent to him for that purpose so long as he provided the necessary information in written form.

[6] *Francis v DPP* [2004] EWHC 591; (2004) 168 J.P. 492.

[7] *Neal v Fior* [1968] 3 All E.R, 865; *Jacob v Garland* [1974] R.T.R. 40.

The prosecution must prove that the notice of requirement to give information was posted, in accordance with the required procedure.[8]

---

[8] CPR 2005 r.4.2.

Offence	Mode of trial	Section	Imprisonment	Fine	Disqualification	Penalty Points	Endorsement code
Failure of keeper of vehicle, and others to identify driver of vehicle	Summarily	172	No	Level 3	Discretionary if committed otherwise than by virtue of subs.(5) or subs.(11)	3	MS90

Identity of driver, Proof of in summary proceedings

(Reference: Wilkinson's Road Traffic Offences, Ch.7.)

Section 12 of the Road Traffic Offenders Act 1988 permits a court to accept as evidence a written statement from the accused admitting that he was the driver of a vehicle on a particular occasion where he has been served with a notice requiring him to notify the identity of the driver under s.172 of the Road Traffic Act 1988. It is irrelevant that the written statement from the accused to be admitted under this section is in fact a signed copy of the notice sent under s.172.[1] It is open to the defendant to prove that he did not sign the document. The document is merely evidential as to the fact of its contents (albeit fairly persuasive), but not conclusive. It must be open to a defendant to put evidence before the court that someone else was in fact the driver. This might be the case where a husband, wife or partner has been put upon to take responsibility for an offence. Obviously such a reversal in the evidence may lead to further, potentially more serious charges resulting, if accepted.

12 PROOF, IN SUMMARY PROCEEDINGS, OF IDENTITY OF DRIVER OF VEHICLE

(1) Where on the summary trial in England and Wales of an information for an offence to which this subsection applies—

    (a) it is proved to the satisfaction of the court, on oath or in manner prescribed by Criminal Procedure Rules, that a requirement under section 172 of the Road Traffic Act 1988 to give information as to the identity of the driver of a particular vehicle on the particular occasion to which the information relates has been served on the accused by post, and

    (b) a statement in writing is produced to the court purporting to be signed by the accused that the accused was the driver of that vehicle on that occasion, the court may accept that statement as evidence that the accused was the driver of that vehicle on that occasion.

(2) Schedule 1 to this Act shows the offences to which subsection (1) above applies.[2]

Similar provisions apply in relation to proceedings relating to a fixed penalty offence. Where the accused has exercised his right to request a hearing, the signed notice of such request can be admitted in evidence to show that the

---

[1] *Francis v DPP* [2004] EWHC Admin 591; (2004) 168 J.P. 492.
[2] See **Appendix 2**.

defendant was the owner, hirer or driver of the vehicle. It is open to the defendant to prove that he did not sign the document. The document is merely evidential as to the facts, not conclusive.

81   DOCUMENTS SIGNED BY THE ACCUSED

(1) Where—

    (a) any person is charged with a fixed penalty offence, and

    (b) the prosecutor produces to the court a document to which this subsection applies purporting to have been signed by the accused,

the document shall be presumed, unless the contrary is proved, to have been signed by the accused and shall be evidence (and, in Scotland, sufficient evidence) in the proceedings of any facts stated in it tending to show that the accused was the owner, the hirer or the driver of the vehicle concerned at a particular time.

(2) Subsection (1) above applies to any document purporting to be—

    (a) a notice requesting a hearing in respect of the offence charged given in accordance with a fixed penalty notice relating to that offence, or

    (b) a statutory statement of any description defined in Schedule 4 to this Act or a copy of a statement of liability within the meaning of section 66 of this Act provided in response to a notice to owner.

Insurance, Using without

(Reference: Wilkinson's Road Traffic Offences, Ch.10.)

The requirement to be insured in relation to the use of a motor vehicle on a road or other public place is set out in s.143 of the Road Traffic Act 1988.

143 USERS OF MOTOR VEHICLES TO BE INSURED OR SECURED AGAINST THIRD-PARTY RISKS

(1) Subject to the provisions of this Part of this Act—

    (a) a person must not use a motor vehicle on a road or other public place unless there is in force in relation to the use of the vehicle by that person such a policy of insurance or such a security in respect of third party risks as complies with the requirements of this Part of this Act, and

    (b) a person must not cause or permit any other person to use a motor vehicle on a road or other public place unless there is in force in relation to the use of the vehicle by that other person such a policy of insurance or such a security in respect of third party risks as complies with the requirements of this Part of this Act.

(2) If a person acts in contravention of subsection (1) above he is guilty of an offence.

(3) A person charged with using a motor vehicle in contravention of this section shall not be convicted if he proves—

    (a) that the vehicle did not belong to him and was not in his possession under a contract of hiring or of loan,

    (b) that he was using the vehicle in the course of his employment, and

    (c) that he neither knew nor had reason to believe that there was not in force in relation to the vehicle such a policy of insurance or security as is mentioned in subsection (1) above.

(4) This Part of this Act does not apply to invalid carriages.

Section 144 of the Road Traffic Act sets out certain exceptions to the general requirement for the use of all vehicles to be insured. These exceptions relate to vehicles owned by public bodies, such as council vehicles, ambulances, police vehicles, etc.

The requirement is to have a policy of insurance, or a security, in respect of third party risks. That policy must have been delivered to the assured[1] although

---

[1] Road Traffic Act 1988 s.147(1).

if an insurance company regards itself as "on risk" a prosecution would not normally be pursued.

For the meaning of "using" or "causing or permitting to use" see **Causing, permitting, using**.

The offence is one of strict liability and the burden of proving of insured use switches to the defendant once the prosecutor has established the defendant's use of, or causing or permitting use of, a vehicle on a road or other public place. The defendant is required to show on the balance of probabilities that the use of the vehicle was covered by a valid certificate of insurance.[2] It is not clear whether, if the defendant produces a certificate of insurance, it is for the prosecution to prove beyond reasonable doubt that the certificate did not in fact provide cover.[3] Although proof by way of producing a valid certificate covering the vehicle on the date and at the time in question should suffice, lack of production of such a policy is not fatal, and the court must consider the other evidence available, including evidence from the defendant himself and any correspondence from his insurance company.

Knowledge as to whether the use was covered by insurance is not relevant. Honest and genuine belief that the vehicle was insured is no defence.

It is not necessary for the user of the vehicle to be the owner or registered keeper. Any person using a vehicle without insurance will be committing an offence.

There is a statutory defence under s.143(3) where a defendant can prove he was driving:

a) a vehicle that did not belong to him and was not in his possession under a contract of hire or loan;

b) that he was using the vehicle in the course of his employment; and

c) that he did not know or have reason to believe that the vehicle was not insured.

The burden of proof is on the defendant, to the balance of probabilities.

There is an extended time period for commencing prosecution of these summary offences; six months from the date on which the offence came to the prosecutor's knowledge, subject to an overall time limit of three years from the commission of the offence.

---

[2] Magistrates' Courts Act 1980 s.101.
[3] Left open in *Howey v Bradley* [1970] Crim. L.R. 223.

Insurance: penalties

Offence	Mode of trial	Section	Imprisonment	Level of fine	Disqualification	Penalty points	Endorsement code	Sentencing guidelines
No insurance	Summary	s.143	—	Level 5	Discretionary	6–8	IN10	Fine Band C. Court should carefully consider whether to disqualify.
Failing to produce insurance certificate	Summary	s.165(1)	—	Level 3	—	—		

No insurance	Road Traffic Act 1988, s.143

Triable only summarily:
Maximum penalty: Level 5 fine

Must endorse and may disqualify. If no disqualification, impose 6-8 points – see notes below.

OFFENCE SERIOUSNESS (CULPABILITY AND HARM)
A. IDENTIFY THE APPROPRIATE STARTING POINT
Starting points based on first time offender pleading not guilty

Examples of nature of activity	Starting point	Range
Using a motor vehicle on a road or other public place without insurance	Band C fine	Band C fine 6 points – 12 months disqualification – see notes below

OFFENCE SERIOUSNESS (CULPABILITY AND HARM)
B. CONSIDER THE EFFECT OF AGGRAVATING AND MITIGATING FACTORS
(OTHER THAN THOSE WITHIN EXAMPLES ABOVE)

Common aggravating and mitigating factors are identified in the pullout card. The following may be particularly relevant but these lists are not exhaustive:

Factors indicating higher culpability	Factors indicating lower culpability
1. Never passed test	1. Responsibility for providing insurance rests with another
2. Gave false details	2. Genuine misunderstanding
3. Driving LGV, HGV, PSV etc.	3. Recent failure to renew or failure to transfer vehicle details where insurance was in existence
4. Driving for hire or reward	4. Vehicle not being driven
5. Evidence of sustained uninsured use	
Factor indicating greater degree of harm	
1. Involved in accident	
2. Accident resulting in injury	

FORM A PRELIMINARY VIEW OF THE APPROPRIATE SENTENCE, THEN CONSIDER OFFENDER MITIGATION
Common factors are identified in the pullout card

CONSIDER A REDUCTION FOR GUILTY PLEA

CONSIDER ANCILLARY ORDERS
Refer to pages 142-148 for guidance on available ancillary orders

DECIDE SENTENCE

GIVE REASONS

Notes

Consider range from 7 points – 2 months disqualification where vehicle was being driven and no evidence that the offender has held insurance.

Consider disqualification of 6 – 12 months if evidence of sustained uninsured use and/or involvement in accident.

Licence, Full and provisional entitlement

(Reference: Wilkinson's Road Traffic Offences, Ch.11.)

There are two parts to the modern driving licence, a photocard and the paper counterpart. Both parts of the licence must be produced to the court when a defendant is under a duty to do so, as required by s.7 of the Road Traffic Offenders Act 1988.

7 DUTY OF ACCUSED TO PROVIDE LICENCE

(1) A person who is prosecuted for an offence involving obligatory or discretionary disqualification and who is the holder of a licence must—

    (a) cause it to be delivered to the proper officer of the court not later than the day before the date appointed for the hearing, or

    (b) post it, at such a time that in the ordinary course of post it would be delivered not later than that day, in a letter duly addressed to the clerk and either registered or sent by the recorded delivery service, or

    (c) have it with him at the hearing

and the foregoing obligations imposed on him as respects the licence also apply as respects the counterpart to the licence.

(2) In subsection (1) above "proper officer" means—

    (a) in relation to a magistrates' court in England and Wales, the designated officer for the court, and

    (b) in relation to any other court, the clerk of the court.

The defendant facing an offence carrying obligatory or discretionary disqualification is required to ensure that both parts of his licence, the photocard and the counterpart, have reached the court the day before the hearing, or to bring them with him to the hearing.

Where the licence is not produced as required, then unless he satisfies the court that he had applied for a new licence and has not received it, not only is he is guilty of an offence, but more importantly, his licence is "suspended" from the time when its production was required until it is produced, complete with counterpart. During the period of suspension, the licence is "of no effect"[1] and presumably a defendant driving in such circumstances is liable to be prosecuted for the offence of driving without a licence.

---

[1] Road Traffic Offenders Act 1988 s.27.

Driving without a licence

A holder of a provisional licence must comply with the conditions attached to the provisional licence, namely to be supervised by a suitably qualified driver and to have L-plates on the vehicle. Anyone driving otherwise than in accordance with a licence authorising driving of a motor vehicle of that class will be committing the offence of driving without a licence.

87 DRIVERS OF MOTOR VEHICLES TO HAVE DRIVING LICENCES

(1) It is an offence for a person to drive on a road a motor vehicle of any class otherwise than in accordance with a licence authorising him to drive a motor vehicle of that class.

(2) It is an offence for a person to cause or permit another person to drive on a road a motor vehicle of any class otherwise than in accordance with a licence authorising that other person to drive a motor vehicle of that class.

Revocation of licence

Where a licence has been "revoked", any person who drives without first applying for a new licence to be issued will be committing the offence of driving without a licence under s.87 of the Road Traffic Act 1988.

A licence is automatically revoked where a court imposes a disqualification of 56 days or more, the revocation taking effect from the beginning of the period of disqualification. Shorter periods of disqualification do not result in automatic revocation and at the end of the disqualification period, the original licence has effect again.

Driving licences: penalties

Offence	Mode of trial	Section	Imprisonment	Level of fine	Disqualification	Penalty points	Endorsement code	Sentencing guidelines
Driving otherwise than in accordance with licence	Summary	s.87(1)	—	Level 3	Discretionary if offence is committed by driving a motor vehicle in a case where either no driving licence for driving that vehicle could have been granted to offender, or where offender is under age, or unsupervised in vehicle as "L" driver, or without "L" plates as an "L" driver, or a learner motor cyclist carrying a passenger	6–8	LC20	Fine Band A

Offence	Mode of trial	Section	Imprisonment	Level of fine	Disqualification	Penalty points	Endorsement code	Sentencing guidelines
Causing or permitting a person to drive otherwise than in accordance with driving licence	Summary	s.87(2)	—	3	—	—	—	—
Failure to deliver licence revoked by virtue of s.92(7A) to Secretary of State	Summary	s.92(7C)	—	3	—	—	—	—
Driving after making false declaration as to physical fitness	Summary	s.92(10)	—	4	Discretionary	3–6	LC30	—
Failure to deliver revoked licence to Secretary of State	Summary	s.93(3)	—	3	—	—	—	—
Driving after failure to notify Secretary of State	Summary	s.94(3A)	—	3	Discretionary	3–6	LC40	—

Offence	Mode of trial	Section	Imprisonment	Level of fine	Disqualification	Penalty points	Endorsement code	Sentencing guidelines
Driving after refusal of licence under s.92(3) or revocation under s.93	Summary	s.94A	6 months or level 5 or both		Discretionary	3-6	LC50	—
Failing to sign licence	Summary	Motor Vehicles (Driving Licences) Regs and s.91 RTOA 1988	—	3	—	—	—	—
Failing to produce driving licence, etc., or state date of birth	Summary	s.164	—	3	—	—	—	—
Failing to produce licence to court	Summary	s.27 RTOA 1988	—	3	—	—	—	—
Failing to produce Northern Ireland driving licence to court	Summary	s.109	—	3	—	—	—	—
Failing to give date of birth	Summary	s.25 RTOA 1988	—	3	—	—	—	—
Applying for or obtaining a licence without disclosing current endorsement	Summary	s.45 RTOA 1988	—	3	—	—	—	—

Mechanically propelled vehicle, Motor Vehicle, Meaning of

(Reference: Wilkinson's Road Traffic Offences, Ch.1.)

A "motor vehicle" is defined in the Road Traffic Act 1988 s.185 as a mechanically propelled vehicle intended or adapted for use on roads. (Note that there are varying definitions in other statutes.)

For a vehicle to come within the definition in s.185 of the Act, it must be "mechanically propelled". The term covers petrol and oil driven vehicles, and in addition steam-driven and electrically driven vehicles.[1]

A vehicle which has previously been mechanically propelled will remain so, until the vehicle has reached such a stage that it can be said that "there is no reasonable prospect of the vehicle ever being made mobile again".[2] The onus of proof that a vehicle had ceased to be mechanically propelled is on the defence so long as it resembled an ordinary motor vehicle.

---

[1] See Wilkinson's Road Traffic Offences, 1.04–1.54 for a more detailed discussion. In *DPP v King* [2008] EWHC 447 (Admin) a "City Mantis" electric scooter was a motor vehicle as defined by the Road Traffic Act 1988 s.185 as a reasonable person might regard the use of the scooter on a public road as something that might well occur.

[2] *Binks v Department of the Environment* [1975] R.T.R. 318, approving earlier authorities.

Notice of intended prosecution, Requirement to give

(Reference: Wilkinson's Road Traffic Offences, Ch.2.)

The Road Traffic Offenders Act s.1 provides as follows:

1 REQUIREMENT OF WARNING, ETC. OF PROSECUTIONS FOR CERTAIN OFFENCES

(1) Subject to section 2 of this Act, a person shall not be convicted of an offence to which this section applies unless—

(a) he was warned at the time the offence was committed that the question of prosecuting him for some one or other of the offences to which this section applies would be taken into consideration, or

(b) within fourteen days of the commission of the offence a summons (or, in Scotland, a complaint) for the offence was served on him, or

(c) within fourteen days of the commission of the offence a notice of the intended prosecution specifying the nature of the alleged offence and the time and place where it is alleged to have been committed, was—

(i) in the case of an offence under section 28 or 29 of the Road Traffic Act 1988 (cycling offences), served on him,

(ii) in the case of any other offence, served on him or on the person, if any, registered as the keeper of the vehicle at the time of the commission of the offence.

(1A) A notice required by this section to be served on any person may be served on that person—

(a) by delivering it to him;

(b) by addressing it to him and leaving it at his last known address; or

(c) by sending it by registered post, recorded delivery service or first class post addressed to him at his last known address.

(2) A notice shall be deemed for the purposes of subsection (1)(c) above to have been served on a person if it was sent by registered post or recorded delivery service addressed to him at his last known address, notwithstanding that the notice was returned as undelivered or was for any other reason not received by him.

(3) The requirement of subsection (1) above shall in every case be deemed to have been complied with unless and until the contrary is proved.

(4) Schedule 1 to this Act shows the offences to which this section applies.

2   REQUIREMENT OF WARNING, ETC.: SUPPLEMENTARY

(1) The requirement of section 1(1) of this Act does not apply in relation to an offence if, at the time of the offence or immediately after it, an accident occurs owing to the presence on a road of the vehicle in respect of which the offence was committed.

(2) The requirement of section 1(1) of this Act does not apply in relation to an offence in respect of which—

 (a) a fixed penalty notice (within the meaning of Part III of this Act) has been given or fixed under any provision of that Part, or
 (b) a notice has been given under section 54(4) of this Act.

(3) Failure to comply with the requirement of section 1(1) of this Act is not a bar to the conviction of the accused in a case where the court is satisfied—

 (a) that neither the name and address of the accused nor the name and address of the registered keeper, if any, could with reasonable diligence have been ascertained in time for a summons or, as the case may be, a complaint to be served or for a notice to be served or sent in compliance with the requirement, or
 (b) that the accused by his own conduct contributed to the failure.

(4) Failure to comply with the requirement of section 1(1) of this Act in relation to an offence is not a bar to the conviction of a person of that offence by virtue of the provisions of—

 (a) section 24 of this Act, or
 (b) any of the enactments mentioned in section 24(6);

 but a person is not to be convicted of an offence by virtue of any of those provisions if section 1 applies to the offence with which he was charged and the requirement of section 1(1) was not satisfied in relation to the offence charged.

The Act, requires that for certain offences:

(a) the defendant must have been warned at the time that he might be prosecuted;

(b) a summons must have been served within 14 days of the offence; or

(c) a notice of intended prosecution must have been sent by the prosecutor within 14 days of the offence.

The offences to which s.1 applies are set out in Sch.1 to the 1988 Offenders Act (see Appendix 2) and include the following:

Dangerous driving;

Careless driving;

Speeding (including temporary limits);

Failing to comply with traffic directions and signs;

Leaving a vehicle in a dangerous position.

Only one of the requirements of s.1 need be fulfilled, and charging a defendant within 14 days of the offence will satisfy the requirements.[1]

The notice of intended prosecution may be sent to the driver or to the registered keeper of the vehicle.

A failure to meet the requirements will prevent conviction of the offence to which it applies. The requirements under s.1 do not apply if the offending vehicle is the cause of an accident at the time, or shortly thereafter.[2]

---

[1] *Sage v Townsend*, The Times, May 27, 1986.

[2] *R. v (1) Myers (2) Ennis-Simpson* [2007] EWCA Crim 599. The exception in s.2 of the Road Traffic Offenders Act 1988 applied where the accident was attributed to the presence of a vehicle on the road, not to the fact that its driver committed a road traffic offence. However, the policy of the section required there to be a sufficient causal link between the offence and the accident that the driver did not need to be warned of the risk of prosecution. Applying that analysis, there was a sufficient causal link between B's fatal accident and the presence on the road of the vehicles that M and E were driving dangerously. All three of them were driving dangerously and one of them crashed his car.

Procedure

(Reference: Wilkinson's Road Traffic Offences, Ch.2.)

Commencement of proceedings

All criminal proceedings commence in the magistrates' court. This is either in the form of the defendant being arrested, charged and produced or bailed to appear before the court, or on the laying of an information followed by the issue of a summons.[1]

Time limits for commencing prosecutions

There is no time limit for commencing prosecutions for offences triable only on indictment or triable either-way.[2] These will nearly always be commenced by way of charge, with the defendant being bailed to appear before the magistrates' court. Prosecutions for some either-way offences may be commenced by way of summons (e.g. dangerous driving, possession of a document with intent to deceive), but for these offences, the defendant must attend for the purpose of indicating his plea (see later), and if not present at the hearing date, the court must adjourn and require his attendance, or issue a warrant to secure his attendance.[3]

Prosecutions for summary offences are subject to jurisdictional time limits. The general rule is that summary proceedings must be commenced within six months of the date of the commission of the alleged offence. However, s.6 of the Road Traffic Offenders Act 1988 extends the period for certain offences[4] by providing that the six month period commences on the date on which evidence sufficient in the opinion of the prosecutor to warrant proceedings came into his knowledge.[5] There is a statutory bar on these offences being prosecuted more than three years after the offence. The prosecutor is required to provide a signed certificate stating the date on which such evidence came to his knowledge, and will be conclusive evidence of that fact.

---

[1] A simplified procedure for commencing proceedings is on the statute book, but as yet there is no identified date for it being brought into force.

[2] Offences triable either way are offences that must be tried in the Crown Court, if the magistrates so direct or the defendant elects, or may be tried in the magistrates' court if the magistrates consider the offence suitable and the defendant consents.

[3] See s.1 and s.13 of the Magistrates' Courts Act 1980.

[4] Including offences of aiding and abetting the specified offences.

[5] *Swan v Vehicle Inspectorate* (1996) 161 J.P. 293; [1997] R.T.R. 187, a person authorised to investigate but not to prosecute is not a prosecutor for the purpose of this section. Time does not start to run until a person authorised to prosecute becomes aware of the evidence.

The Road Traffic Offenders Act 1988 s.6:

6 TIME WITHIN WHICH SUMMARY PROCEEDINGS FOR CERTAIN OFFENCES MUST BE COMMENCED

(1) Subject to subsection (2) below, summary proceedings for an offence to which this section applies may be brought within a period of six months from the date on which evidence sufficient in the opinion of the prosecutor to warrant the proceedings came to his knowledge.

(2) No such proceedings shall be brought by virtue of this section more than three years after the commission of the offence.

(3) For the purposes of this section, a certificate signed by or on behalf of the prosecutor and stating the date on which evidence sufficient in his opinion to warrant the proceedings came to his knowledge shall be conclusive evidence of that fact.

(4) A certificate stating that matter and purporting to be so signed shall be deemed to be so signed unless the contrary is proved.

(5) In relation to proceedings in Scotland, subsection (3) of section 136 of the Criminal Procedure (Scotland) Act 1995 (date of commencement of proceedings) shall apply for the purposes of this section as it applies for the purposes of that.

(6) Schedule 1 to this Act shows the offences to which this section applies.

The offences in Sch.1 (see **Appendix 2**) include driving or obtaining a licence whilst disqualified, using, or causing or permitting use without insurance, and various offences in connection with failure to notify the Secretary of State of a disability or driving when a licence has been revoked for disability, etc.

Procedure for indictable-only[6] offences

These offences cannot be dealt with in a magistrates' court and must be "sent" to the crown court. "Sending" is a straight-forward process anticipated to take place at the first hearing. The court may also "send" any offences triable either-way or summarily, provided that they are related to the indictable-only offence and in the case of summary offences, are imprisonable or involve obligatory or discretionary disqualification from driving.[7] The magistrates' court may specify the Crown Court to which offences are sent and make preliminary directions with regard to case management.

---

[6] Indictable offences are offences that can only be tried in the Crown Court.
[7] s.51(11) of the Crime and Disorder Act 1998.

Procedure for either-way offences

For offences that can be tried either way, the procedure under s.17A to s.20 of the Magistrates' Courts Act will apply as follows.[8]

1. The defendant will first be asked to indicate his intended plea to the offence.

2. Before he gives that indication, he must be informed by the court of the fact that indication of a guilty plea will result in conviction in the magistrates' court and the loss of a right to trial in the crown court, although the power to commit for sentence to that court remains.

3. Where a defendant indicates his intention to plead not guilty, or declines to indicate any plea, the court will determine whether the matter is more suitable for trial in the magistrates' court, or whether the trial should take place at the crown court. That decision will be based on the prosecution summary of the facts, the prosecution case to be taken at the highest. It is not open to the defence to seek to persuade the court to retain jurisdiction on the basis that the facts are less serious than put by the prosecution. If the court concludes that, in the event of conviction, its powers of sentence would be insufficient, or for some other good reason the case should be tried at the crown court, jurisdiction will be declined. If however, the magistrates indicate that they would be prepared to accept jurisdiction, summary trial can only take place if the defendant so consents. Otherwise, he is entitled to elect trial by jury.

4. Where the magistrates indicate the matter is suitable for summary trial the defendant will be warned again that consenting to summary trial does not prevent subsequent committal to the crown court for sentence in the event of conviction in the magistrates' court. He will then be asked whether he elects trial at the crown court, or consents to trial in the magistrates' court.

5. In the event of the magistrates deciding the matter is not suitable for summary trial, or the defendant electing trial in the crown court, the proceedings will need to be adjourned for a committal hearing under s.6 of the Magistrates' Courts Act 1980.

6. In the event that the magistrates find the matter suitable for summary trial and the defendant consents, his formal plea to the offence(s) will be taken and if a not guilty plea is entered,[9] the court will move on to deal with matters of case management and list the matter for trial.

---

[8] Note that for these offences the prosecutor will be required to provide advance information under the CPR 2005 if requested by a defendant. (See **Disclosure**.)

[9] Note that from this point, the Criminal Procedure and Investigations Act 1996 applies in relation to disclosure, and the standard directions issued under the consolidated Practice Direction will apply. (See **Disclosure**.)

Procedure for summary only offences

If the defendant is present, the charge will be read to him and he will be asked to enter his plea. If the defendant is absent, the court will be informed if he has entered a guilty plea by post.[10] Where no plea has been entered, the prosecutor may seek to proceed with the hearing in the absence of the defendant. If the magistrates are satisfied that the defendant is aware of the date of the hearing and that it is appropriate to proceed in absence, the prosecutor may put before the court the prosecution evidence in the form of statements that comply with the required provisions of s.9 of the Criminal Justice Act 1967,[11] or call oral evidence. If the statements are to be relied upon, the court will need to be satisfied that they have been served on the defendant at least seven days before the date of the hearing. If the magistrates decline to proceed in the absence of the defendant, they should adjourn to give notice to the defendant that he must attend.

Following conviction, magistrates may not disqualify a defendant in his absence without first adjourning and giving notice of their intention to impose such an order and affording the defendant the opportunity to attend and make representations. If having given the required notice, a defendant fails to attend an adjourned hearing, the magistrates may proceed to make such an order, or issue a warrant for the defendant's arrest.[12]

Defendant unaware of proceedings

A defendant who was genuinely unaware of proceedings before the court may make a statutory declaration under s.14 of the Magistrates' Courts Act 1980. That declaration will be that he did not know of the summons or proceedings until a date specified in the declaration, being a date after the court has begun to try the information. The declaration must be served on the designated officer for the court within 21 days of that date. A court[13] may accept late service of such a declaration where it appears that it was not reasonable to expect the accused to serve the declaration within the 21 day period. The effect of a statutory declaration is to make "void" the summons and all subsequent proceedings. The summons may be re-issued and the proceedings commenced afresh. No issue will arise over time limits as it is only the summons that is made void, not the originating information.

The court also has a power under s.142 of the Magistrates' Courts Act 1980 to re-open cases to rectify mistakes.[14] These powers include not only the power to set aside a **sentence or order** if it appears invalid, but also if it appears to the

---

[10] See **Guilty plea, Written notification of.**
[11] These statements must be signed by the maker, contain the required declaration as to the truth of the contents, copies must have been served on the defendant, and the defendant must not have notified his objection to the statements being relied upon within seven days from the date of service of a copy of the statement; see s.9(2) of the Criminal Justice Act 1967.
[12] See ss.11 and 13 of the Magistrates' Courts Act 1980.
[13] For this purpose, a court may be comprised of a single justice.
[14] There is no time limit, but such applications should be made within a reasonable time.

court to be in the interests of justice to do so.[15] Section 142(2), (2A) and (3) allow a court, where it is in the interests of justice to do so, to set aside a **conviction** and direct that a case should be heard again before different justices. In such circumstances, the proceedings are not "void", but to be treated as if the trial had been adjourned.

---

[15] It will be very rare that a court will exercise this power to increase a sentence, other than to correct a clear mistake (e.g. where the increased penalty is mandatory). See *R. (on the application of Holme) v Liverpool City Justices and Crown Prosecution Service* [2004] EWHC 3131; (2005) 169 J.P. 306.

Road, Meaning of

(Reference: Wilkinson's Road Traffic Offences, Ch.1.)

The definition of "Road" appears in the Road Traffic Act 1988 s.192(1). "Road" means any highway and any other road to which the public has access and includes bridges over which a road passes.

There are similar definitions in other relevant statutes, although note that the Vehicle Excise and Registration Act 1994 is restricted to vehicles on "public roads", i.e. repairable at public expense.

Note that some offences are committed "on a road or other public place" clearly indicating that the public place need not be a road.

The burden is on the prosecution to prove that the offence is committed on a "road" within the definition of the Act. This is likely to be a matter of fact and degree and courts have decided that a pavement is a road even though part of the pavement was in private ownership[1]; a vehicle is on a road where it is partly on the road and partly on private land[2]; a vehicle is "on" a road even if it could not be said to be in actual physical contact with the road surface[3]; where fencing has been put up with reference to the highway, there is a rebuttable presumption that the highway extends to the whole space between the fencing[4]; a footpath or bridleway that can properly be described as a highway will come within the definition of "road".[5] It does not matter that the road is a cul-de-sac or not made up.[6] A car park is not a "road" even if the general public have access to it. Roads and car parks have separate and distinct characters. A road requires there to be a definable route or way with ascertainable edges, leading from one point to another with the function of allowing travellers to move along that route. In contrast, the function of a car park is to enable vehicles to stand and wait.[7]

A "highway" is a public right of way including footpaths, bridleways, driftways, carriageways and footways. A full highway provides the public with a right of way including vehicles.[8] There should be some evidence of permanent dedication of the highway to the public.

The prosecution will need to establish that the general public has access to the road, not merely a special class of the general public. That access may be by tolerance of the owner or proprietor of the road, the test for which is whether access is obtained by overcoming a physical obstruction or in defiance of

---

[1] *Price v DPP* [1990] R.T.R. 413.
[2] *Randall v Motor Insurers' Bureau* [1969] 1 All E.R. 21.
[3] *Holliday v Henry* [1974] R.T.R. 101, where a roller skate was interposed between each wheel and the surface of the road.
[4] *Att-Gen v Beynon* [1969] 2 All E.R. 263.
[5] *Lang v Hindhaugh* [1986] R.T.R. 271.
[6] *Bass v Boynton* [1960] Crim. L.R. 497.
[7] *Cutter v Eagle Star Insurance Co Ltd, Clarke v Kato* [1998] 4 All E.R. 417.
[8] *Suffolk CC v Mason* [1979] 2 All E.R. 369 at 371.

prohibition, express or implied.[9] The fact that a notice identifies a road as "private" is not conclusive.[10] The forecourt of a hotel used as a short cut by members of the public, even though private property with no access as of right, in the absence of any obstruction separating it from the highway, was held to be a road.[11] A forecourt of a shop with no obstruction separating it from the highway was not a road as there was no evidence of use by the public other than customers of the shop.[12]

---

[9] Dictum of Lord Sands in *Harrison v Hill* 1932 J.C. 13 at 17, approved in *Cox v White* [1976] R.T.R. 248.

[10] *Hogg v Nicholson* [1968] S.L.T. 265, a road marked "private" serving a few houses also used by persons from a neighbouring village visiting the sub-post office, was still a road to which the public had access.

[11] *Bugge v Taylor* (1940) 104 J.P. 467.

[12] *Thomas v Dando* [1951] 1 All E.R. 1010.

Sentencing, General principles

(Reference: Wilkinson's Road Traffic Offences, Ch.13.)

A sentence may not exceed the maximum penalty set for the offence, or the jurisdiction of the court.[1] Sentences will take into account any guidance from higher courts set out in the case-law, and any relevant guidance issued by the Sentencing Guidelines Council[2] and must pay attention to any decisions of the Court of Appeal[3] confirming advice from the Council. The Magistrates' Courts Sentencing Guidelines provide guidance to be followed in the magistrates' courts.[4]

The factual basis on which the offender is to be sentenced must be clear. This will normally be provided to the court by the prosecutor outlining the facts of the offence, upon which the defence must have an opportunity to comment. The court should be informed of any matters which tend to make the offence more serious (aggravating features) or less serious (mitigating features).

Where a plea has been entered on the basis of a particular set of facts, these facts should be recorded in writing and signed by the offender and prosecutor.[5] If there is a dispute as to the factual basis of an offence, it may be necessary for there to be a "Newton hearing"[6] for the court to establish the facts. This will only be necessary if the difference in the facts alleged by the prosecution and defence would make a material difference to sentence.[7] It is a matter for the court whether or not to hold such a hearing.[8] Where a "Newton hearing" is not required, the court should make clear the basis on which it is sentencing[9] and any doubts should be resolved in favour of the offender[10] unless manifestly false[11] or wholly implausible[12] such that the court is entitled to reject them.[13]

The prosecutor will also inform the court as to the offender's character and antecedents. This will normally be in the form of a printout from the Police National Computer. It should be borne in mind that these are not always up-to-date. The court will also require an offender to produce any relevant driving

---

[1] The jurisdiction of the magistrates' court is limited to six months' imprisonment in total, unless the court is dealing with at least two offences triable either-way when the maximum increases to 12 months. See s.133(2) of the Magistrates' Courts Act 1980. A Youth Court has a maximum jurisdiction of two years detention regardless of the nature of the offence(s).

[2] Section 172 of the Criminal Justice Act 2003 requires a court to take the guidelines into account unless there is a good and sufficient reason to depart from them.

[3] *R. v Johnson* [1994] Crim. L.R. 537.

[4] Revised guidelines are due to be issued in October 2008 by the Sentencing Guidelines Council.

[5] See the comprehensive guidance given in *R. v Underwood and other appeals* [2004] All E.R. (D) 575.

[6] *R. v Newton* (1983) 77 Cr.App.R. 13.

[7] *R. v Sweeting* [1988] Crim. L.R. 131.

[8] *R. v Pearce* (1979) 1 Cr.App.R.(S.) 317.

[9] *R. v Brown* [1982] Crim. L.R. 53.

[10] *R. v Taggart* (1979) 1 Cr.App.R.(S.) 144.

[11] *R. v Hawkins* (1985) 7 Cr.App.R.(S.) 351.

[12] *R. v Palmer* (1994) 15 Cr.App.R.(S.) 123.

[13] *R. v Tolera* [1998] Crim. L.R. 425.

licence where the offence carries obligatory endorsement. Where a licence is not available, it may be possible for the court to obtain information directly from the DVLA, but this service is becoming increasingly restricted and may require the case to be adjourned. See **Licence, full and provisional entitlement** for the consequences of not producing a licence on conviction.

There are various statutory requirements that courts must take into account when sentencing that may require the court to increase severity of the penalty by making the offence more serious, or to reduce the penalty by way of mitigation.

1. Any racial or religious aggravation must be treated as increasing the seriousness of the offence and therefore be reflected in an increase in the severity of the sentence.[14]

2. An offence committed whilst on bail increases the seriousness of the offence and therefore requires the court to increase the severity of the sentence.[15]

3. The court must consider whether to give a discount for an early guilty plea; the sentencing guidelines give very specific guidance as to what that discount should be.[16]

Many magistrates' courts are using a written pro forma to aid their sentencing decision. This is based on the sentencing requirements imposed under the Criminal Justice Act 2003 and the guidance issued by the Sentencing Guidelines Council (see below).

The structured approach is a three stage process.

1. The first consideration is to assess the seriousness of the offence, taking into account aggravating and mitigating features and forming a view of the culpability of the defendant and the risk of harm posed by his offending.[17] At this stage the magistrates will make a preliminary decision as to where the offence fits under the guidance in the magistrates courts guidelines. Where the magistrates court guidelines indicate a level of penalty (discharge or fine, community penalty or custody), that level is based on offences of average seriousness. If the

---

[14] s.145 of the Crime and Disorder Act 1998.

[15] s.143(3) of the Criminal Justice Act 2003.

[16] See Sentencing Guidelines—dealing with reductions for a guilty plea *R. v Bowering* [2005] EWCA Crim 3215; it is not appropriate to reduce the usual discount on the basis that a defendant has been caught red-handed, nor because the maximum penalty for the offence is considered to be too low. *R v Barney* [2007] EWCA Crim 3181; offenders could not always expect to receive a reduction in sentence for genuine remorse and a guilty plea, particularly where those offenders had earlier sought to reduce their culpability through fictitious defence statements before entering those pleas.

[17] Relevant previous convictions, racial or religious aggravation, offending on bail, failure to respond to previous sentences should be taken into account at this stage as aggravating features that serve to increase the seriousness of the offence. Mitigation about the offence is also to be taken into account at this stage, but not mitigation about the offender.

magistrates have determined this offence to be above or below the average, they will need to consider whether to move away from the guideline penalty indicated.

2. The next consideration is to take into account any offender mitigation, such as difficult domestic circumstances or genuine remorse. These must not be mitigating factors to do with the offence which will already have been taken into account in fixing the level of seriousness. Offender mitigation can only serve to reduce the severity of any penalty. Magistrates may not increase severity at this stage. There may be no offender mitigation, or none that the court considers relevant. The magistrates should at this stage consider the appropriate sentence, which may remain the same as their preliminary consideration, or may be reduced by way of offender mitigation.

3. The third stage is to consider any appropriate reduction for a guilty plea and to fix any ancillary orders, such as endorsement or disqualification, costs, compensation.

Standard Scale Fines

Level on the standard scale	Maximum fine
1	£200
2	£500
3	£1,000
4	£2,500
5	£5,000

SENTENCING STRUCTURE

1.	**OFFENCE SERIOUSNESS (CULPABILITY AND HARM)**
A.	<u>**IDENTIFY THE APPROPRIATE STARTING POINT**</u>

- Consider which of the examples of offence activity corresponds most closely to the circumstances of the case to identify the appropriate **starting point**.
- Starting points are based on a **first time offender pleading not guilty**.
- Refer to the following where starting point is, or **range** includes, a:
  - (i)   fine;
  - (ii)   community order;
  - (iii)   custodial sentence.
- Refer to Guidelines for the meaning of the terms 'starting point', 'range' and 'first time offender'.

1.	**OFFENCE SERIOUSNESS (CULPABILITY AND HARM)**
B.	<u>**CONSIDER THE EFFECT OF AGGRAVATING AND MITIGATING FACTORS**</u>

- Move up or down from the starting point to reflect aggravating or mitigating factors that affect the seriousness of the offence to reach a provisional sentence.
- Common aggravating and mitigating factors are set out overleaf; relevant factors are also identified in the individual offence guidelines. **These lists are not exhaustive.**
- Do not double-count any aggravating or mitigating factors in the description of the activity used to reach the starting point.
- The **range** is the bracket into which the provisional sentence will normally fall but the court is not precluded from going outside the range where the facts justify it.
- Previous convictions which aggravate the seriousness of the current offence may take the provisional sentence beyond the range, especially if there are significant other aggravating factors present.

2.	**FORM A PRELIMINARY VIEW OF THE APPROPRIATE SENTENCE, THEN CONSIDER OFFENDER MITIGATION**

- Matters of offender mitigation may include remorse and admissions to police in interview.

3.	**CONSIDER A REDUCTION FOR A GUILTY PLEA**

- Apply the sliding scale reduction for a guilty plea to punitive elements of the sentence.
- Application of the reduction may take the sentence below the range in some cases.

4.	**CONSIDER ANCILLARY ORDERS, INCLUDING COMPENSATION**

- Refer to Guidelines for guidance on available ancillary orders.
- Consider compensation in every case where the offending has resulted in personal injury, loss or damage – give reasons if order not made.

5.	**DECIDE SENTENCE**
	GIVE REASONS

- Review the total sentence to ensure that it is proportionate to the offending behaviour and properly balanced.
- Give reasons for the sentence passed, including any ancillary orders.
- State if the sentence has been reduced to reflect a guilty plea; indicate what the sentence would otherwise have been.
- Explain if the sentence is of a different kind or outside the range indicated in the guidelines.

SENTENCING FORM   **MAGISTRATES' COURT**

A: PRE-SENTENCE ASSESSMENT STAGE

DATE: [ ]   **1a) DEFENDANT:** [ ]

b) D.O.B: [ ]   **c) ADDRESS:** [ ]

2. CUSTODY: [ ]   **BAIL:** [ ]

3. CHARGES: [ ]

4. SENTENCING STARTING POINT AND RANGE

Discharge Fine A	Discharge Fine B	Discharge Fine C	Comm Low	Comm Medium	Comm High	Custody 6 wks	Custody 12 wks	Custody 18 wks	Commit to Cr Ct

5. OFFENCE FACTORS INFLUENCING ASSESSMENT

a) Aggravating factors	b) Mitigating factors

c) Culpability: intentional [ ]   reckless [ ]   knew likely outcome [ ]   negligent [ ]

d) Harm caused/risked: [ ]

6. OFFENDER FACTORS INFLUENCING ASSESSMENT

[ ]

7. SERIOUSNESS ASSESSMENT

Discharge Fine A	Discharge Fine B	Discharge Fine C	Comm Low	Comm Medium	Comm High	Custody 6 wks	Custody 12 wks	Custody 18 wks	Commit to Cr Ct

8. MAIN (1) AND SECONDARY (2) PURPOSE(S) OF SENTENCE

Punishment [ ]   Rehabilitation [ ]   Reduction in crime/ deterrence [ ]   Protection of public [ ]   Reparation [ ]

9. COMMUNITY ORDER REQUIREMENTS TO BE INVESTIGATED (Ensure that the defendant is warned that this does not guarantee a non-custodial sentence will be imposed)

[ ]

10. REPORT TYPE: Fast [ ]   Standard [ ]   Due: [ ]

B: SENTENCING STAGE

11. FACTORS ARISING FROM REPORT
Including, if appropriate, a) why you have reached a different conclusion from the indications of seriousness and purpose already given, or b) why you are departing from the proposals in the report.

12. SENTENCE TO BE IMPOSED (referring to reasons)

13. CREDIT FOR GUILTY PLEA
Record a) the extent of credit given and reasons for it, or b) what the sentence would have been if a timely guilty plea had been entered. (NB: Do not double count credit – see note 6 in guidance on completion).

14. ANCILLARY ORDERS
Details of compensation (or reasons for not awarding it), plus other ancillary orders.

15. REASONS FOR DEPARTING FROM SENTENCING COUNCIL GUIDELINES

16. EXPLAIN SENTENCE USING APPROPRIATE PRONOUNCEMENTS

Remitting an offender to another court

A magistrates' court may remit an offender to another magistrates' court for sentence where:

a) the offender is aged 18 years or more and has been convicted of the offence(s) to be remitted;

b) the offences are punishable with imprisonment or driving disqualification;

c) the court to which the offender is to be remitted has also convicted the offender of an offence punishable with imprisonment or driving disqualification, which has not yet been dealt with, and consents to the remittal.[1]

Committal for sentence

The court has power to commit a defendant to the crown court for sentence for an offence triable either-way, if it is of the opinion that the offence, or the offence and one or more of the offences associated with it is so serious that its powers of punishment are insufficient.[2] When committing for sentence for such an offence, the court may also commit for sentence any offence whatsoever of which the defendant has been convicted.[3] Note that this section is often mis-read as restricting ancillary committal of summary offences when committing an either-way offence, to those which carry imprisonment or disqualification under s.34, s.35 or s.36 of the Road Traffic Offenders Act 1988, as set out in s.6(3). However, s.6(3) only applies where the "relevant offence" being committed for sentence is a summary offence. Where the "relevant offence" is an either way offence, s.6(2) applies and no such restriction is stated.

When committing a defendant to the crown court, the magistrates may remand the defendant on bail or in custody.

---

[1] See s.10 of the Powers of the Criminal Courts (Sentencing) Act 2000.
[2] See s.3 of the Powers of the Criminal Courts (Sentencing) Act 2000.
[3] See s.6(2) of the Powers of Criminal Courts (Sentencing) Act 2000.

Sentencing, Magistrates' Courts guidelines

The revised Magistrates' Courts Sentencing guidelines issued by the Sentencing Guidelines Council give suggested penalties for offences. The guidelines themselves explain how they should be used and copies of current guidelines are available from the Sentencing Guidelines Council website.[1]

Every court is under a statutory obligation to have regard to any relevant Council guideline.[2] If a court imposes a sentence of a different kind or outside the range indicated in a Council guideline, it is obliged to state its reasons for doing so.[3]

Where individual guidelines are available for particular offences, they are included in the section dealing with that offence. Incorporated in this section are guidelines issued for more minor road traffic offences appropriate for the imposition of a fine or discharge.

See **Sentencing, general principles** for further information.

---

[1] *http://www.sentencing-guidelines.gov.uk/guidelines/index.html* [Accessed May 14, 2008].
[2] Criminal Justice Act 2003 s.172(1).
[3] Criminal Justice Act 2003 s.174(2)(a).

OFFENCES APPROPRIATE FOR IMPOSITION OF FINE OR DISCHARGE

PART 1: OFFENCES CONCERNING THE DRIVER

OFFENCE	MAX. PEN.	POINTS	STARTING POINT	SPECIAL CONSIDERATIONS
Fail to co-operate with preliminary (roadside) breath test	L3	4	B	
Fail to give information of driver's identity as required	L3	6	C	For limited companies, endorsement is not available; a fine is the only available penalty.
Fail to produce insurance certificate	L4	–	A	Fine per offence, not per document
Fail to produce test certificate	L3	–	A	
Drive otherwise than in accordance with licence (where could be covered)	L3	–	A	
Drive otherwise than in accordance with licence	L3	3–6	A	Aggravating factor if no licence ever held

PART 2: OFFENCES CONCERNING THE VEHICLE

* The guidelines for some of the offences below differentiate between three types of offender when the offence is committed in the course of business: driver, owner-driver and owner-company. **Where the offender is an owner-driver, the starting point is the same as for a driver; however, the court should consider an uplift of at least 25%.**

OFFENCE	MAX. PEN.	POINTS	STARTING POINT	SPECIAL CONSIDERATIONS
No excise licence	L3 or 5 times annual duty, whichever is greater	–	A (1–3 months unpaid) B (4–6 months unpaid) C (7–12 months unpaid)	Add duty lost
Fail to notify change of ownership to DVLA	L3	–	A	If offence committed in course of business: A (driver) A* (owner-driver) B (owner-company)
No test certificate	L3	–	A	If offence committed in course of business: A (driver) A* (owner-driver) B (owner-company)
Brakes defective	L4	3	B	If offence committed in course of business: B (driver) B* (owner-driver) C (owner-company) L5 if goods vehicle— see Part 5 below
Steering defective	L4	3	B	If offence committed in course of business: B (driver) B* (owner-driver) C (owner-company) L5 if goods vehicle— see Part 5 below

Tyres defective	L4	3	B	If offence committed in course of business: B (driver) B* (owner-driver)C (owner-company) L5 if goods vehicle— see Part 5 below Penalty per tyre
Condition of vehicle/ accessories/equipment involving danger of injury (s.40A, Road Traffic Act 1988)	L4	3	B	Must disqualify for at least 6 months if offender has one or more previous convictions for same offence within three years If offence committed in course of business: B (driver) B* (owner-driver) C (owner-company) L5 if goods vehicle— see Part 5 below
Exhaust defective	L3	–	A	If offence committed in course of business: A (driver) A* (owner-driver) B (owner-company)
Lights defective	L3	–	A	If offence committed in course of business: A (driver) A* (owner-driver) B (owner-company)

PART 3: OFFENCES CONCERNING USE OF VEHICLE

* The guidelines for some of the offences below differentiate between three types of offender when the offence is committed in the course of business: driver, owner-driver and owner-company. **Where the offender is an owner-driver, the starting point is the same as for a driver; however, the court should consider an uplift of at least 25%.**

OFFENCE	MAX. PEN.	POINTS	STARTING POINT	SPECIAL CONSIDERATIONS
Weight, position or distribution of load or manner in which load secured involving danger of injury (s.40A, Road Traffic Act 1988)	L4	3	B	Must disqualify for at least 6 months if offender has one or more previous convictions for same offence within three years If offence committed in course of business: A (driver) A* (owner-driver) B (owner-company) L5 if goods vehicle— see Part 5 below

Number of passengers or way carried involving danger of injury (s.40A, Road Traffic Act 1988)	L4	3	B	If offence committed in course of business: A (driver) A* (owner-driver) B (owner-company) L5 if goods vehicle—see Part 5 below
Position or manner in which load secured (not involving danger) (s.42, Road Traffic Act 1988)	L3	–	A	L4 if goods vehicle—see Part 5 below
Overloading / exceeding axle weight	L5	–	A	Starting point caters for cases where the overload is up to and including 10%. Thereafter, 10% should be added to the penalty for each additional 1% of overload Penalty per axle If offence committed in course of business: A (driver) A* (owner-driver) B (owner-company) If goods vehicle—see Part 5 below
Dangerous parking	L3	3	A	
Pelican/zebra crossing contravention	L3	3	A	
Fail to comply with traffic sign (e.g. red traffic light, stop sign, double white lines, no entry sign)	L3	3	A	
Fail to comply with traffic sign (e.g. give way sign, keep left sign, temporary signs)	L3	–	A	
Fail to comply with police constable directing traffic	L3	3	A	
Fail to stop when required by police constable	L5 (mechanically propelled vehicle) L3 (cycle)	–	B	
Use of mobile telephone	L3	3	A	
Seat belt offences	L2 (adult or child in front) L2 (child in rear)	–	A	
Fail to use appropriate child car seat	L2	–	A	

PART 4: MOTORWAY OFFENCES

OFFENCE	MAX. PEN.	POINTS	STARTING POINT	SPECIAL CONSIDERATIONS
Drive in reverse or wrong way on slip road	L4	3	B	
Drive in reverse or wrong way on motorway	L4	3	C	
Drive off carriageway (central reservation or hard shoulder)	L4	3	B	
Make U turn	L4	3	C	
Learner driver or excluded vehicle	L4	3	B	
Stop on hard shoulder	L4	–	A	
Vehicle in prohibited lane	L4	3	A	
Walk on motorway, slip road or hard shoulder	L4	–	A	

PART 5: OFFENCES RE BUSES / GOODS VEHICLES OVER 3.5 TONNES (GVW)

* The guidelines for these offences differentiate between three types of offender: driver; owner-driver; and owner-company. **Where the offender is an owner-driver, the starting point is the same as for a driver; however, the court should consider an uplift of at least 25%.**

** In all cases, take safety, damage to roads and commercial gain into account. Refer to page 125 for approach to fines for 'commercially motivated' offences.

OFFENCE	MAX. PEN.	POINTS	STARTING POINT	SPECIAL CONSIDERATIONS
No goods vehicle plating certificate	L3	–	A (driver) A* (owner-driver) B (owner-company)	
No goods vehicle test certificate	L4	–	B (driver) B* (owner-driver) C (owner-company)	
Brakes defective	L5	3	B (driver) B* (owner-driver) C (owner-company)	
Steering defective	L5	3	B (driver) B* (owner-driver) C (owner-company)	
Tyres defective	L5	3	B (driver) B* (owner-driver) C (owner-company)	Penalty per tyre
Exhaust emission	L4	–	B (driver) B* (owner-driver) C (owner-company)	
Condition of vehicle/ accessories/equipment involving danger of injury (s.40A, Road Traffic Act 1988)	L5	3	B (driver) B* (owner-driver) C (owner-company)	Must disqualify for at least 6 months if offender has one or more previous convictions for same offence within three years

Number of passengers or way carried involving danger of injury (s.40A, Road Traffic Act 1988)	L5	3	B (driver) B* (owner-driver) C (owner-company)	Must disqualify for at least 6 months if offender has one or more previous convictions for same offence within three years
Weight, position or distribution of load or manner in which load secured involving danger of injury (s.40A, Road Traffic Act 1988)	L5	3	B (driver) B* (owner-driver) C (owner-company)	Must disqualify for at least 6 months if offender has one or more previous convictions for same offence within three years
Position or manner in which load secured (not involving danger) (s.42, Road Traffic Act 1988)	L4	–	B (driver) B* (owner-driver) C (owner-company)	
Overloading/exceeding axle weight	L5	–	B (driver) B* (owner-driver) C (owner-company)	Starting points cater for cases where the overload is up to and including 10%. Thereafter, 10% should be added to the penalty for each additional 1% of overload Penalty per axle
No operators licence	L4	–	B (driver) B* (owner-driver) C (owner-company)	
Speed limiter not used or incorrectly calibrated	L4	–	B (driver) B* (owner-driver) C (owner-company)	
Tachograph not used/not working	L5	–	B (driver) B* (owner-driver) C (owner-company)	
Exceed permitted driving time/ periods of duty	L4	–	B (driver) B* (owner-driver) C (owner-company)	
Fail to keep/return written record sheets	L4	–	B driver) B* (owner-driver) C (owner-company)	
Falsify or alter records with intent to deceive	L5/2 years	–	B (driver) B* (owner-driver) C (owner-company)	Either way offence

Special reasons, not to disqualify/endorse, and mitigating circumstances

(Reference: Wilkinson's Road Traffic Offences, Ch.21.)

Special reasons are reasons upon which a court may refrain from disqualifying in respect of an offence carrying obligatory disqualification, or from endorsing points in respect of an offence carrying obligatory endorsement.

Mitigating circumstances are circumstances in which a court may, under a wider discretion, refrain from disqualifying when considering a penalty points disqualification.

In both cases, the finding of special reasons or mitigating circumstances does not entitle a defendant to escape disqualification or endorsement, it merely means that the court has a discretion to exercise in that respect; the court is not bound to exercise that discretion and in an appropriate case will not do so.

Special reasons

There is no statutory definition of what amounts to a special reason. Whether a matter is capable of being a special reason is a question of law. The generally accepted definition is that to amount to a special reason, a matter must:

1) be a mitigating or extenuating circumstance;

2) not amount in law to a defence charged;

3) be directly connected with the commission of the offence; and

4) be one which the court ought properly to take into consideration.[1]

Although the special reason must be directly connected with the commission of the offence, a submission that the offence was not a serious one will not suffice.[2]

A circumstance peculiar to the offender, not related to the offence, cannot amount to a special reason.[3]

The following are examples of what courts have found to be a special reason:

a) shortness of distance driven where the vehicle was unlikely to come into contact with other road users;

b) unintentional commission of an offence, without negligence;

c) offending while coping with a true emergency.

---

[1] *R. v Wickens* (1958) 42 Cr.App.R. 236.
[2] *Nicholson v Brown* [1974] R.T.R. 177.
[3] *DPP v Murray* [2001] EWHC Admin 848; where a defendant was ignorant of the fact that a motorised scooter was in law a mechanically propelled vehicle.

The following are examples of what courts have found not to be a special reason:

- a) good character, good driving record, likely personal or financial hardship;
- b) defendant is a doctor, or holds some other employment of benefit to the public which requires him to have a licence;
- c) the fact that the defendant has already been prevented from driving for some time before sentence by a condition of bail;
- d) the offence itself was not serious.

The burden of proof is on the defendant to establish that a special reason exists, on the balance of probabilities. Special reasons must be supported by admissible evidence; submissions made on behalf of a defendant by an advocate will not suffice.[4]

Where special reasons are found in the case of obligatory disqualification, and the court decides to exercise its discretion, it may decide not to disqualify at all, or to impose a shorter period of disqualification than the obligatory minimum period. Additionally, the court can exercise its discretion not to endorse any points which would be required to be endorsed if no disqualification is imposed.

Where special reasons are found in the case of obligatory endorsement, the court's discretion if it decides to exercise it, is confined to not endorsing any points.

Where the court finds special reasons established, these must be stated in court and entered on the register.

Special reasons in relation to offences of using without insurance

Ignorance of cover, or the limited nature of the cover provided by a policy of insurance is not normally a special reason,[5] but can be if there is a good reason for ignorance of the extent of the policy, or if the defendant was misled.

Special reasons in relation to offences of drink/driving

Special reasons caused by an illness or drug, the effects of which are not known to a defendant cannot amount to a special reason.[6] Nor can a defendant claim that he was mistaken as to the amount of alcohol he had in fact drunk.[7]

Special reasons can be found where a defendant was:

- a) unaware he was consuming alcohol;

---

[4] *Jones v English* [1951] 2 All E.R. 853.
[5] *Rennison v Knowler* [1947] 1 All E.R. 302; an honest but groundless belief that the policy covered a particular use cannot amount to a special reason.
[6] *Kinsall v DPP* [2002] EWHC Admin 545.
[7] *Newnham v Trigg* [1970] R.T.R. 107.

b) aware he was consuming alcohol but deceived or misled as to the nature of the drink.

The defendant will need to show that

a) his drink was laced;

b) he did not know or suspect that his drink was laced;

c) if his drink had not been laced, the alcohol level in his blood would not have exceeded the prescribed limit.[8]

These facts will need to be established by admissible evidence. A defendant giving evidence that he has now been told that someone had spiked his drinks will usually be insufficient, as his account of the lacing of the drinks will be hearsay.

The case law shows that courts will generally expect a defendant to show that he had done all that he could reasonably be expected to do to avoid the commission of an offence.[9]

Although belching at the time of providing a breath specimen resulting in a risk of inflated reading cannot amount to a defence to the offence of drink/driving (see **Driving, or attempting to drive, over the prescribed limit**), it may be capable of founding a special reason.[10]

In drink/drive cases, even where a special reason is established, the court must take into account the level of the reading or the degree of impairment when considering whether to exercise a discretion not to disqualify. In laced drinks cases, the court will take into account whether the defendant should have realised that he was not fit to drive.[11]

When considering special reasons in relation to offences of failing to provide a specimen, factors relating to the decision to drive, or shortness of distance driven, etc. cannot be relevant as they do not relate to the offence before the court.[12] Although the offence itself requires the prosecution to have proved no reasonable excuse exists for the failure to provide, this does not mean that special reasons cannot be found.[13]

Emergency

A sudden medical emergency could justify driving so as to be capable of amounting to a special reason.[14] A defendant will have to show that there was no

---

[8] *Pugsley v Hunter* [1973] R.T.R. 284. Unless obvious to a layman, c) will need to be established by calling medical or scientific evidence.

[9] *Robinson v DPP* [2003] EWHC 2718; [2004] Crim. L.R. 670.

[10] *Ng v DPP* [2007] EWHC 36 (Admin). Expert evidence is almost certainly required to establish such a special reason.

[11] *Pridige v Grant* [1985] R.T.R. 196.

[12] *Anderton v Anderton* [1977] R.T.R. 424.

[13] *Daniels v DPP* [1992] R.T.R. 140.

[14] *Brown v Dyerson* [1969] 1 Q.B. 45. Note that such a reason might also be capable of amounting to a defence of duress of circumstance, as per Simon Brown L.J. in *DPP v Whittle* [1996] R.T.R. 154.

alternative but to drive, and that every reasonable alternative had been considered. The emergency must be real and not something that the defendant should have anticipated arising.

Shortness of distance driven

Shortness of the distance driven as a special reason has been confined to situations where the vehicle was unlikely to come into contact with other road users. Seven matters are required to be considered:[15]

1) how far the vehicle was driven;

2) in what manner it was driven;

3) the state of the vehicle;

4) whether the driver intended to go further;

5) the road and traffic conditions prevailing at the time;

6) whether there was a possibility of danger by coming into contact with other road users or pedestrians; and

7) what the reason was for the car being driven.

It is suggested that the key question to be considered by the court is what would a sober, reasonable and responsible non-driver friend of the defendant, present at the time, have advised in the circumstances; drive or not drive?[16]

Mitigating circumstances

Mitigating circumstances are applicable only to the discretion not to disqualify a defendant liable to a penalty points disqualification.

Under s.35 of the Road Traffic Offenders Act 1988, the court must order disqualification for not less than the minimum period unless the court is satisfied, having regard to all the circumstances, that there are grounds for mitigating the normal consequences of the conviction and thinks fit to order him to be disqualified for a shorter period or not to order him to be disqualified. However, no account is to be taken of any of the following circumstances:

(a) any circumstances that are alleged to make the offence or any of the offences not a serious one;

(b) hardship, other than exceptional hardship[17]; or

---

[15] *Chatters v Burke* [1986] 3 All E.R. 168.

[16] *DPP v Bristow* [1998] R.T.R. 100.

[17] For hardship to be exceptional, it must be more than is normally suffered. Most orders for disqualification will result in some hardship. The exceptional hardship may be to someone other than the offender: *Cornwall v Coke* [1976] Crim. L.R. 519.

(c) any circumstances which, within the three years immediately preceding the conviction, have been taken into account under that subsection in ordering the offender to be disqualified for a shorter period or in not ordering him to be disqualified.[18]

It is for the court to determine if there are mitigating circumstances.

What may amount to mitigating circumstances is wider than may amount to a special reason, and includes matters relating to the offender.

Where a court finds mitigating circumstances and as a result imposes no disqualification, or a lesser period than the minimum required, this must be stated in open court and entered on the court register.

The burden of proof is on the defendant to establish that mitigating circumstances exist. The submission should be supported by admissible evidence: submissions made on behalf of a defendant by an advocate will not usually suffice.

---

[18] The defendant will need to establish that the circumstances are different from a previous finding.

Speeding

(Reference: Wilkinson's Road Traffic Offences, Ch.6.)

Offences of exceeding the speed limit are covered by the Road Traffic Regulation Act 1984. There are four types of offence:

a) exceeding the 20, 30, 40 or 50 mph limit on a restricted road;

b) exceeding temporary limits of 70, 60 or 50 mph on roads other than motorways;

c) exceeding the limit applicable to that class of vehicle (irrespective of type of road);

d) exceeding the limit applicable only on motorways.

The Road Traffic Regulation Act 1984 s.89 creates the offence of speeding:

(1) A person who drives a motor vehicle on a road at a speed exceeding a limit imposed by or under any enactment to which this section applies shall be guilty of an offence.

The section applies to any enactment in the Road Traffic Regulation Act itself, s.2 of the Parks Regulation (Amendment) Act 1926 and any enactment not contained in the Road Traffic Regulation Act but passed after September 2, 1960. However, it does not include offences relating to special roads and offences relating to motorway speed limits (other than for special classes of vehicle) covered by s.17(4) of the Road Traffic Regulation Act.

Exemptions are provided for fire and rescue authority, ambulance and police vehicles when being used for that purpose if observing the speed limit would hinder that use of the vehicle.[1] The exemption is limited to offences of speeding, and will not afford a defence to other road traffic offences, such as careless or dangerous driving.

The defence of necessity, coercion or duress is applicable to road traffic offences and is not limited to deliberate threats from a third party but can include a contingency such as a natural disaster or illness, and includes a situation where the threatened danger is to someone other than the accused. However, the defence will only be available where the circumstances are found to have constrained the accused to act in breach of the law.[2]

In addition to the usual requirement to prove the identity of the driver, and the fact of a motor vehicle being driven on a road the prosecution will need to

---

[1] Road Traffic Regulation Act s.87.

[2] *Moss v Howdle* 1997 S.L.T. 782; where the driver did not need to speed to the next service station, but should have driven onto the hard shoulder to identify the nature of the apparent emergency.

prove the statutory limit for the particular road[3] and that the vehicle speed exceeded that statutory limit.

By s.89(2) of the Road Traffic Regulation Act, a person prosecuted for speeding shall not be convicted solely on the opinion evidence of one witness that the defendant was exceeding the limit.[4] The corroborative evidence must relate to the same time. Usually it will be provided by a speed testing device.

Specific provision for admissibility of evidence in relation to speeding offences, etc.

Section 20 of the Road Traffic Offenders Act 1988 makes specific provision for the admission in evidence of a record produced by a prescribed device, and in the same or another document, of a certificate as the circumstances in which the record was produced signed by a police constable.

A "prescribed device" is one of a description specified in an order made by the Secretary of State.

Section 20(6) states that the evidence of a measurement made by a device, or of the circumstances in which it was made, or that a device was of a type approved, or that any conditions subject to which approval was given were satisfied, may be given by the production of a signed document containing that information.

A copy of that document must be served on the defendant not less than seven days before the hearing or trial. If the defendant requires the attendance of the person who signed the document, notice must be given not less than three days before the hearing or trial.[5]

The provisions of s.20 must be strictly observed. The prosecution must prove that a device is of a type approved before its measurement of a drivers speed can be admitted in evidence.[6] This can be done by producing a copy of the type approval order, or a police officer could give such evidence. However, failure to strictly prove such matters should not be permitted to succeed as an "ambush" defence, and the court will usually allow the prosecution to re-open their case to adduce the relevant evidence where no prior notice was given to the prosecution that the matter was in issue.

20   Speeding Offences, etc: Admissibility of Certain Evidence

(1) Evidence (which in Scotland shall be sufficient evidence) of a fact relevant to proceedings for an offence to which this section applies may be given by the production of—

---

[3] Where the prosecution are put to strict proof of the statutory limit for the road they must provide sufficient proof to meet any statutory requirements. See *Martin v Harrow Crown Court* [2007] EWHC 3193 (Admin) where a police officer suggesting it was "likely" that street lamps were placed not more than 200 yards apart was insufficient.

[4] As this provision only applies to offences created by s.89(1), the requirement for corroboration does not apply to motorway speeding offences created by s.17(4).

[5] A document of such poor quality that it could not be used for the purpose served is not a document served under s.20(8): *Griffiths v DPP* [2007] EWHC 619 (Admin).

[6] *Roberts (Colin) v DPP* [1994] R.T.R. 31.

(a) a record produced by a prescribed device, and

(b) (in the same or another document) a certificate as to the circumstances in which the record was produced signed by a constable or by a person authorised by or on behalf of the chief officer of police for the police area in which the offence is alleged to have been committed;

but subject to the following provisions of this section.

(2) This section applies to—

(a) an offence under section 16 of the Road Traffic Regulation Act 1984 consisting in the contravention of a restriction on the speed of vehicles imposed under section 14 of that Act;

(b) an offence under subsection (4) of section 17 of that Act consisting in the contravention of restriction on the speed of vehicles imposed under that section;

(c) an offence under section 88(7) of that Act (temporary minimum speed limits);

(d) an offence under section 89(1) of that Act (speeding offences generally);

(e) an offence under section 36(1) of the Road Traffic Act 1988 consisting in the failure to comply with an indication given by a light signal that vehicular traffic is not to proceed;

(f) an offence under Part I or II of the Road Traffic Regulation Act 1984 of contravening or failing to comply with an order or regulations made under either of those Parts relating to the use of an area of road which is described as a bus lane or a route for use by buses only;

(g) an offence under section 29(1) of the Vehicle Excise and Registration Act 1994 (using or keeping an unlicensed vehicle on a public road).

(3) The Secretary of State may by order amend subsection (2) above by making additions to or deletions from the list of offences for the time being set out there; and an order under this subsection may make such transitional provision as appears to him to be necessary or expedient.

(4) A record produced or measurement made by a prescribed device shall not be admissible as evidence of a fact relevant to proceedings for an offence to which this section applies unless—

(a) the device is of a type approved by the Secretary of State, and

(b) any conditions subject to which the approval was given are satisfied.

(5) Any approval given by the Secretary of State for the purposes of this section may be given subject to conditions as to the purposes for which, and the manner and other circumstances in which, any device of the type concerned is to be used.

(6) In proceedings for an offence to which this section applies, evidence (which in Scotland shall be sufficient evidence)—

(a) of a measurement made by a device, or of the circumstances in which it was made, or

(b) that a device was of a type approved for the purposes of this section, or that any conditions subject to which an approval was given were satisfied,

may be given by the production of a document which is signed as mentioned in subsection (1) above and which, as the case may be, gives particulars of the measurement or of the circumstances in which it was made, or states that the device was of such a type or that, to the best of the knowledge and belief of the person making the statement, all such conditions were satisfied.

(7) For the purposes of this section a document purporting to be a record of the kind mentioned in subsection (1) above, or to be a certificate or other document signed as mentioned in that subsection or in subsection (6) above, shall be deemed to be such a record, or to be so signed, unless the contrary is proved.

(8) Nothing in subsection (1) or (6) above makes a document admissible as evidence in proceedings for an offence unless a copy of it has, not less than seven days before the hearing or trial, been served on the person charged with the offence; and nothing in those subsections makes a document admissible as evidence of anything other than the matters shown on a record produced by a prescribed device if that person, not less than three days before the hearing or trial or within such further time as the court may in special circumstances allow, serves a notice on the prosecutor requiring attendance at the hearing or trial of the person who signed the document.

(9) In this section "prescribed device" means device of a description specified in an order made by the Secretary of State.

(10) . . .

There is a statutory duty on the Secretary of State or the local authority to erect and maintain signs indicating speed restrictions. Section 85(4) of the Road Traffic Regulation Act 1984 operates to prevent conviction of any motorist for speeding unless the limit is indicated by the required signage. Such signs must be visible to the approaching motorist in sufficient time to enable him to reduce his speed to the new limit.[7]

---

[7] *Coombes v DPP* [2006] EWHC 3263.

Speed limits: penalties

Offence	Mode of trial	Section	Imprisonment	Level of fine	Disqualification	Penalty points	Endorsement code
Exceeding general speed limit for road	Summary	s.89	—	3	Discretionary	3–6	SP30
Exceeding speed limit for goods vehicles	Summary	s.89	—	3	Discretionary	3–6	SP10
Exceeding speed limit for type of vehicle	Summary	s.89	—	3	Discretionary	3–6	SP20
Exceeding speed limit for passenger vehicles	Summary	s.89	—	3	Discretionary	3–6	SP40
Exceeding overall speed limit for motorway	Summary	s.17(4)	—	4	Discretionary	3–6	SP50
Exceeding lower speed limit for vehicle on motorway	Summary	s.89	—	3	Discretionary	3–6	SP10, SP20 or SP40 as appropriate
Temporary speed restriction for roadworks, etc.	Summary	s.16(1)	—	3	Discretionary	3–6	SP60
Minimum speed limit	Summary	s.88(7)	—	3	—	—	—

Road Traffic Regulation Act 1984, s.89(10)	**Speeding**

Triable only summarily:
Maximum penalty: Level 3 fine (level 4 if motorway)

Must endorse and may disqualify. If no disqualification, impose 3–6 points

OFFENCE SERIOUSNESS (CULPABILITY AND HARM) **A. IDENTIFY THE APPROPRIATE STARTING POINT** **Starting points based on first time offender pleading not guilty**			
Speed limit (mph)	Recorded speed (mph)		
20	21-30	31-40	41-50
30	31-40	41-50	51-60
40	41-55	56-65	66-75
50	51-65	66-75	76-85
60	61-80	81-90	91-100
70	71-90	91-100	101-110
Starting point	**Band A fine**	**Band B fine**	**Band B fine**
Range	**Band A fine**	**Band B fine**	**Band B fine**
Points/ disqualification	**3 points**	**4 – 6 points OR Disqualify 7–28 days**	**Disqualify 7–56 days OR 6 points**

OFFENCE SERIOUSNESS (CULPABILITY AND HARM)
B. CONSIDER THE EFFECT OF AGGRAVATING AND MITIGATING FACTORS
(OTHER THAN THOSE WITHIN EXAMPLES ABOVE)
Common aggravating and mitigating factors are identified in the pullout card. The following may be particularly relevant but these lists are not exhaustive:

Factors indicating higher culpability	Factor indicating lower culpability
1. Poor road or weather conditions 2. LGV, HGV, PSV etc. 3. Towing caravan / trailer 4. Carrying passengers or heavy load 5. Driving for hire or reward 6. Evidence of unacceptable standard of driving over and above speed Factors indicating greater degree of harm 1. Location, e.g. near school 2. High level of traffic or pedestrians in the vicinity	1. Genuine emergency established

FORM A PRELIMINARY VIEW OF THE APPROPRIATE SENTENCE, THEN CONSIDER OFFENDER MITIGATION
Common factors are identified in the pullout card

CONSIDER A REDUCTION FOR GUILTY PLEA

CONSIDER ANCILLARY ORDERS
Refer to pages 142-148 for guidance on available ancillary orders

DECIDE SENTENCE

GIVE REASONS

Part 2:

Appendices

Appendix 1

Table of endorsable offences

The following table sets out all the endorsable offences, their penalty points value and whether or not they are obligatorily disqualifiable.

Offence	Legislative provision	Number of penalty points	Disqualification
Manslaughter (or in Scotland culpable homicide) by driver of a motor vehicle	(common law)	3–11[1]	Obligatory
	1988 Act		
Causing death by dangerous driving	s.1	3–11[1]	Obligatory
Dangerous driving	s.2	3–11[1]	Obligatory
Careless or inconsiderate driving	s.3	3–9	Discretionary
Causing death by careless driving when under influence of drink or drugs	s.3A	3–11[1]	Obligatory
Driving or attempting to drive when unfit through drink or drugs	s.4(1)	3–11[1]	Obligatory
Being in charge when unfit through drink or drugs	s.4(2)	10	Discretionary
Driving or attempting to drive with excess alcohol	s.5(1)(a)	3–11[1]	Obligatory
In charge with excess alcohol	s.5(1)(b)	10	Discretionary
Failing or refusing to provide breath for preliminary test	s.6(4)	4	Discretionary
Failing or refusing to provide specimens for analysis when driving or attempting to drive	s.7(6)	3–11[1]	Obligatory
Failing or refusing to provide specimens for analysis when not driving or attempting to drive	s.7(6)	10	Discretionary

Offence	Legislative provision	Number of penalty points	Disqualification
Failing to allow specimen to be subjected to laboratory test when driving or attempting to drive	s.7A	3–11[1]	Obligatory
Failing to allow specimen to be subjected to laboratory test when not driving or attempting to drive	s.7A	10	Discretionary
Motor racing or speed trials on highway	s.12	3–11[1]	Obligatory
Leaving motor vehicle in dangerous position	s.22	3	Discretionary
Carrying passenger on motor cycle other than astride and on a seat	s.23	3	Discretionary
Failing to comply with traffic directions or signals in respect of motor vehicle[2]	ss.35, 36	3	Discretionary
Using vehicle in dangerous condition	s.40(A)	3	Obligatory
Breach of requirement as to control of vehicle, mobile telephones, etc.	s.41A	3	Discretionary
Breach of requirement as to control of vehicle, mobile telephones, etc.	s.41D	3	Discretionary
Driving otherwise than in accordance with a licence	s.87(1)	3–6	Discretionary
Driving after making false declarations as to physical fitness	s.92(10)	3–6	Discretionary
Driving after failure to notify disability	s.94(3A)	3–6	Discretionary
Driving after refusal or revocation of licence	s.94A	3–6	Discretionary
Driving with uncorrected defective eyesight	s.96(1)	3	Discretionary
Refusing eyesight test	s.96(3)	3	Discretionary
Driving while disqualified by court order	s.103(1)(b)	6	Discretionary
Using motor vehicle whilst uninsured	s.143	6–8	Discretionary
Failing to stop after accident	s.170(4)	5–10	Discretionary
Failing to give particulars or report accident	s.170(4)	5–10	Discretionary
Failure to give information as to identity of driver	s.172	3	Discretionary
Taking, etc., a motor vehicle in Scotland without authority	s.178	6	Discretionary

Offence	Legislative provision	Number of penalty points	Disqualification
Theft Act 1968			
Stealing or attempting to steal a motor vehicle	s.1		Discretionary
Taking or attempting to take, etc., a motor vehicle without authority	s.12		Discretionary
Aggravated vehicle-taking	s.12A	3–11[1]	Obligatory
Going equipped for stealing or for taking motor vehicles	s.25		Discretionary
RTR Act 1984			
Contravention of temporary speed restriction	s.16(1)	3–6 or 3 (fixed penalty)	Discretionary
Motorway offences	s.17(4)	3–6 or 3 (fixed penalty) if speeding, otherwise 3	Discretionary
Pedestrian crossing offence in respect of motor vehicle	s.25	3	Discretionary
School crossing patrol offence in respect of motor vehicle	s.28	3	Discretionary
Street playground offence in respect of motor vehicle	ss.29. 30	2	Discretionary
Speeding offences	s.89	3–6 or 3 (fixed penalty)	Discretionary
RTO Act 1988			
Aiding and abetting, etc., an obligatorily disqualifiable offence	s.28(1)(b)	10	Discretionary
Aiding or abetting, etc., an endorsable offence			Discretionary
Attempting to commit an endorsable offence			Discretionary

[1] No penalty points may be imposed when the offender is disqualified.
[2] Certain traffic signs only.

Appendix 2

SCHEDULE 1 ROAD TRAFFIC OFFENDERS ACT 1988

SCHEDULE 1 OFFENCES TO WHICH SECTIONS 1, 6, 11 AND 12(1) APPLY

Section 1

1

(1) Where section 1, 6, 11 or 12(1) of this Act is shown in column 3 of this Schedule against a provision of the Road Traffic Act 1988 specified in column 1, the section in question applies to an offence under that provision.

(2) The general nature of the offence is indicated in column 2.

1A

Section 1 also applies to—

    (a) an offence under section 16 of the Road Traffic Regulation Act 1984 consisting in the contravention of a restriction on the speed of vehicles imposed under section 14 of that Act,

    (b) an offence under subsection (4) of section 17 of that Act consisting in the contravention of a restriction on the speed of vehicles imposed under that section, and

    (c) an offence under section 88(7) or 89(1) of that Act (speeding offences).

2

Section 6 also applies—

    (a) to an offence under section 67 of this Act, . . .

    (b) in relation to Scotland, to an offence under section 173 of the Road Traffic Act 1988 (forgery, etc, of licences, test certificates, certificates of insurance and other documents and things) [, . . .

    (c) . . .] and [

    (d) to an offence under paragraph 3(5) of Schedule 1 to the Road Traffic (New Drivers) Act 1995].

3

Section 11 also applies to—

    (a) any offence to which section 112 of the Road Traffic Regulation Act 1984 (information as to identity of driver or rider) applies except an offence under section 61(5) of that Act,

(b) any offence which is punishable under section 91 of this Act, . . .

(bb) . . . and

(c) any offence against any other enactment relating to the use of vehicles on roads.

4

Section 12(1) also applies to—

(a) any offence which is punishable under section 91 of this Act, . . .

[(aa) . . . and]

(b) any offence against any other enactment relating to the use of vehicles on roads.

SCHEDULE 2—PUNISHMENT OF OFFENCES

PART I OFFENCES UNDER THE TRAFFIC ACTS

(1) Provision creating offence	(2) General nature of offence	(3) Mode of prosecution	(4) Punishment	(5) Disqualification	(6) Endorsement	(7) Penalty points
Offences under the Road Traffic Regulation Act 1984						
RTRA section 5	Contravention of traffic regulation order	Summarily	Level 3 on the standard scale			
RTRA section 8	Contravention of order regulating traffic in Greater London	Summarily	Level 3 on the standard scale			
RTRA section 11	Contravention of experimental traffic order	Summarily	Level 3 on the standard scale			
RTRA section 13	Contravention of experimental traffic scheme in Greater London	Summarily	Level 3 on the standard scale			
RTRA section 16(1)	Contravention of temporary prohibition or restriction	Summarily	Level 3 on the standard scale	Discretionary if committed in respect of a speed restriction	Obligatory if committed in respect of a speed restriction	3–6 or 3 (fixed penalty)
[RTRA section 16C(1)	Contravention of prohibition or restriction relating to relevant event	Summarily	Level 3 on the standard scale			
RTRA section 17(4)	Use of special road contrary to scheme or regulations	Summarily	Level 4 on the standard scale	Discretionary if committed in respect of a motor vehicle otherwise than by unlawfully stopping or allowing the vehicle to remain at rest on a part of a special road on which vehicles are in certain circumstances permitted to remain at rest	Obligatory if committed as mentioned in the entry in column 5	3–6 or 3 (fixed penalty) if committed in respect of a speed restriction, 3 in any other case

Section	Offence	Mode	Punishment	Disqualification	Endorsement	Points
RTRA section 18(3)	One-way traffic on trunk road	Summarily	Level 3 on the standard scale			
RTRA section 20(5)	Contravention of prohibition or restriction for roads of certain classes	Summarily	Level 3 on the standard scale			
RTRA section 25(5)	Contravention of pedestrian crossing regulations	Summarily	Level 3 on the standard scale	Discretionary if committed in respect of a motor vehicle	Obligatory if committed in respect of a motor vehicle	3
RTRA section 28(3)	Not stopping at school crossing	Summarily	Level 3 on the standard scale	Discretionary if committed in respect of a motor vehicle	Obligatory if committed in respect of a motor vehicle	3
RTRA section 29(3)	Contravention of order relating to street play-ground	Summarily	Level 3 on the standard scale	Discretionary if committed in respect of a motor vehicle	Obligatory if committed in respect of a motor vehicle	2
RTRA section 35A(1)	Contravention of order as to use of parking place	Summarily	(a) Level 3 on the standard scale in the case of an offence committed by a person in a street parking place reserved for disabled persons' vehicles or in an off-street parking place reserved for such vehicles, where that person would not have been guilty of that offence if the motor vehicle in respect of which it was committed had been a disabled person's vehicle (b) Level 2 on the standard scale in any other case			

(1) Provision creating offence	(2) General nature of offence	(3) Mode of prosecution	(4) Punishment	(5) Disqualification	(6) Endorsement	(7) Penalty points
RTRA section 35A(2)	Misuse of apparatus for collecting charges or of parking device or connected apparatus	Summarily	Level 3 on the standard scale			
RTRA section 35A(5)	Plying for hire in parking place	Summarily	Level 2 on the standard scale			
RTRA section 43(5)	Unauthorised disclosure of information in respect of licensed parking place	Summarily	Level 3 on the standard scale			
RTRA section 43(10)	Failure to comply with term or conditions of licence to operate parking place	Summarily	Level 3 on the standard scale			
RTRA section 43(12)	Operation of public off-street parking place without licence	Summarily	Level 5 on the standard scale			
RTRA section 47(1)	Contraventions relating to designated parking places	Summarily	(a) Level 3 on the standard scale in the case of an offence committed by a person in a street parking place reserved for disabled persons' vehicles where that person would not have been guilty of that offence if the motor vehicle in respect of which was committed had been a disabled person's vehicle (b) Level 2 in any other case			
RTRA section 47(3)	Tampering with parking meter	Summarily	Level 3 on the standard scale			

				Disqualification	Endorsement	Penalty points
				Discretionary	Obligatory	3–6 or 3 (fixed penalty)
RTRA section 52(1)	Misuse of parking device	Summarily	Level 2 on the standard scale			
RTRA section 53(5)	Contravention of certain provisions of designation orders	Summarily	Level 3 on the standard scale			
RTRA section 53(6)	Other contraventions of designation orders	Summarily	Level 2 on the standard scale			
RTRA section 61(5)	Unauthorised use of loading area	Summarily	Level 3 on the standard scale			
RTRA section 88(7)	Contravention of minimum speed limit	Summarily	Level 3 on the standard scale			
RTRA section 89(1)	Exceeding speed limit	Summarily	Level 3 on the standard scale	Discretionary	Obligatory	3–6 or 3 (fixed penalty)
RTRA section 104(5)	Interference with notice as to immobilisation device	Summarily	Level 2 on the standard scale			
RTRA section 104(6)	Interference with immobilisation device	Summarily	Level 3 on the standard scale			
RTRA section 105(5)	Misuse of disabled person's badge (immobilisation devices)	Summarily	Level 3 on the standard scale			
RTRA section 105(6A)	Misuse of recognised badge (immobilisation devices)	Summarily	Level 3 on the standard scale			
RTRA section 108(2) (or that sub-section as modified by section 109(2) and (3))	Non-compliance with notice (excess charge)	Summarily	Level 3 on the standard scale			
RTRA section 108(3) (or that sub-section as modified by section 109(2) and (3))	False response to notice (excess charge)	Summarily	Level 5 on the standard scale			
RTRA section 112(4)	Failure to give information as to identity of driver	Summarily	Level 3 on the standard scale			
RTRA 115(1)	Mishandling or faking parking documents	(a) Summarily (b) On indictment	(a) The statutory maximum (b) 2 years			
RTRA section 115(2)	False statement for procuring authorisation	Summarily	Level 4 on the standard scale			

(1) Provision creating offence	(2) General nature of offence	(3) Mode of prosecution	(4) Punishment	(5) Disqualification	(6) Endorsement	(7) Penalty points
RTRA section 116(1)	Non-delivery of suspect document or article	Summarily	Level 3 on the standard scale			
RTRA section 117	Wrongful use of disabled person's badge	Summarily	Level 3 on the standard scale			
RTRA section 117(1)	Wrongful use of recognised badge	Summarily	Level 3 on the standard scale			
RTRA section 117(1A)		Summarily	Level 3 on the standard scale			
RTRA section 129(3)	Failure to give evidence at inquiry					
Offences under the Road Traffic Act 1988						
RTA section 1	Causing death by dangerous driving	On indictment	14 years	Obligatory	Obligatory	3–11
RTA section 2	Dangerous driving	(a) Summarily (b) On indictment	(a) 6 months or the statutory maximum or both (b) 2 years or a fine or both	Obligatory	Obligatory	3–11
RTA section 3	Careless, and inconsiderate, driving	Summarily	Level 5 on the standard scale	Discretionary	Obligatory	3–9
RTA section 3A	Causing death by careless driving when under influence of drink or drugs	On indictment	14 years or a fine or both	Obligatory	Obligatory	3–11
RTA section 4(1)	Driving or attempting to drive when unfit to drive through drink or drugs	Summarily	6 months or level 5 on the standard scale or both	Obligatory	Obligatory	3–11
RTA section 4(2)	Being in charge of a [mechanically propelled vehicle] when unfit to drive through drink or drugs	Summarily	3 months or level 4 on the standard scale or both	Discretionary	Obligatory	10
RTA section 5(1)(a)	Driving or attempting to drive with excess alcohol in breath, blood or urine	Summarily	6 months or level 5 on the standard scale or both	Obligatory	Obligatory	3–11

RTA section 5(1)(b)	Being in charge of a motor vehicle with excess alcohol in breath, blood or urine	Summarily	3 months or level 4 on the standard scale or both	Discretionary	Obligatory	10
RTA section 6	Failing to co-operate with a preliminary test	Summarily	Level 3 on the standard scale	Discretionary	Obligatory	4
RTA section 7	Failing to provide specimen for analysis or laboratory test	Summarily	(a) Where the specimen was required to ascertain ability to drive or proportion of alcohol at the time offender was driving or attempting to drive, 6 months or level 5 on the standard scale or both (b) In any other case, 3 months or level 4 on the standard scale or both	(a) Obligatory in case mentioned in column 4(a) (b) Discretionary in any other case	Obligatory	(a) 3–11 in case mentioned in column 4(a) (b) 10 in any other case
RTA section 7A	Failing to allow specimen to be subjected to laboratory test	Summarily	(a) Where the test would be for ascertaining ability to drive or proportion of alcohol at the time offender was driving or attempting to drive, 6 months or level 5 on the standard scale or both (b) In any other case, 3 months or level 4 on the standard scale or both	(a) Obligatory in the case mentioned in column 4(a) (b) Discretionary in any other case	Obligatory	(a) 3–11, in case mentioned in column 4(a) (b) 10, in any other case

(1) Provision creating offence	(2) General nature of offence	(3) Mode of prosecution	(4) Punishment	(5) Disqualification	(6) Endorsement	(7) Penalty points
RTA section 12	Motor racing and speed trials on public ways	Summarily	Level 4 on the standard scale	Obligatory	Obligatory	3–11
RTA section 13	Other unauthorised or irregular competitions or trials on public ways	Summarily	Level 3 on the standard scale			
RTA section 14	Driving or riding in a motor vehicle in contravention of regulations requiring wearing of seat belts	Summarily	Level 2 on the standard scale			
RTA section 15(2)	Driving motor vehicle with child not wearing seat belt or with child in a rear-facing child restraint in front seat with an active air bag	Summarily	Level 2 on the standard scale			
RTA Section 15(4)	Driving motor vehicle with child in rear not wearing seatbelt	Summarily	Level 2 on the standard scale			
RTA section 15A(3) or (4)	Selling etc in certain circumstances equipment as conducive to the safety of children in motor vehicles	Summarily	Level 3 on the standard scale			
RTA section 15B	Failure to notify bus passengers of the requirement to wear seat belt	Summarily	Level 4 on the standard scale			
RTA section 16	Driving or riding motor cycles in contravention of regulations requiring wearing of protective headgear	Summarily	Level 2 on the standard scale			

				Disqualification		Penalty points
RTA section 17	Selling, etc, helmet not of the prescribed type as helmet for affording protection for motor cyclists	Summarily	Level 3 on the standard scale			
RTA section 18(3)	Contravention of regulations with respect to use of head-worn appliances on motor cycles	Summarily	Level 2 on the standard scale			
RTA section 18(4)	Selling, etc, appliance not of prescribed type as approved for use on motor cycles	Summarily	Level 3 on the standard scale			
RTA section 19	Prohibition of parking of heavy commercial vehicles on verges, etc	Summarily	Level 3 on the standard scale			
RTA section 21	Driving or parking on cycle track	Summarily	Level 3 on the standard scale			
RTA section 22	Leaving vehicles in dangerous positions	Summarily	Level 3 on the standard scale	Discretionary if committed in respect of a motor vehicle	Obligatory if committed in respect of a motor vehicle	3
RTA section 22A	Causing danger to road-users	(a) Summarily (b) On indictment	(a) 6 months or the statutory maximum or both (b) 7 years or a fine or both			
RTA section 23	Carrying passenger on motor-cycle contrary to section 23	Summarily	Level 3 on the standard scale	Discretionary	Obligatory	3
RTA section 24	Carrying passenger on bicycle contrary to section 24	Summarily	Level 1 on the standard scale			
RTA section 25	Tampering with motor vehicles	Summarily	Level 3 on the standard scale			
RTA section 26	Holding or getting on to vehicle, etc, in order to be towed or carried	Summarily	Level 1 on the standard scale			

(1) Provision creating offence	(2) General nature of offence	(3) Mode of prosecution	(4) Punishment	(5) Disqualification	(6) Endorsement	(7) Penalty points
RTA section 27	Dogs on designated roads without being held on lead	Summarily	Level 1 on the standard scale			
RTA section 28	Dangerous cycling	Summarily	Level 4 on the standard scale			
RTA section 29	Careless, and inconsiderate, cycling	Summarily	Level 3 on the standard scale			
RTA section 30	Cycling when unfit through drink or drugs	Summarily	Level 3 on the standard scale			
RTA section 31	Unauthorised or irregular cycle racing or trials of speed on public ways	Summarily	Level 1 on the standard scale			
RTA section 32	Contravening prohibition on persons under 14 driving electrically assisted pedal cycles	Summarily	Level 2 on the standard scale			
RTA section 33	Unauthorised motor vehicle trial on footpaths or bridle-ways	Summarily	Level 3 on the standard scale			
RTA section 34	Driving mechanically propelled vehicles elsewhere than on roads	Summarily	Level 3 on the standard scale			
RTA section 35	Failing to comply with traffic directions	Summarily	Level 3 on the standard scale	Discretionary, if committed in respect of a motor vehicle by failure to comply with a direction of a constable, traffic officer or traffic warder.	Obligatory if committed as described in column 5	3

RTA section 36	Failing to comply with traffic signs	Summarily	Level 3 on the standard scale	Discretionary, if committed in respect of a motor vehicle by failure to comply with an indication given by a sign specified for the purposes of this paragraph in regulations under RTA section 36	Obligatory if committed as described in column 5	3
RTA section 37	Pedestrian failing to stop when directed by constable regulating traffic	Summarily	Level 3 on the standard scale			
RTA section 40A	Using vehicle in dangerous condition etc	Summarily	(a) Level 5 on the standard scale if committed in respect of a goods vehicle or a vehicle adapted to carry more than eight passengers (b) Level 4 on the standard scale in any other case	[(a) Obligatory if committed within three years of a previous conviction of the offender under section 40A. (b) Discretionary in any other case.	Obligatory	3
RTA section 41A	Breach of requirement as to brakes, steering-gear or tyres	Summarily	(a) Level 5 on the standard scale if committed in respect of a goods vehicle or a vehicle adapted to carry more than eight passengers (b) Level 4 on the standard scale in any other case	Discretionary	Obligatory	3
RTA section 41B	Breach of requirement as to weight: goods and passenger vehicles	Summarily	Level 5 on the standard scale			

(1) Provision creating offence	(2) General nature of offence	(3) Mode of prosecution	(4) Punishment	(5) Disqualification	(6) Endorsement	(7) Penalty points
RTA section 41D	Breach of requirements as to control of vehicle, mobile telephones etc.	Summarily	(a) Level 4 on standard scale if committed in respect of a goods vehicle or a vehicle adapted to carry more than eight passengers (b) Level 3 on the standard scale in any other case			
RTA section 42	Breach of other construction and use requirements	Summarily	(a) Level 4 on standard scale if committed in respect of a goods vehicle or a vehicle adapted to carry more than eight passengers (b) Level 3 on the standard scale in any other case			
RTA section 47	Using, etc, vehicle without required test certificate being in force	Summarily	(a) Level 4 on the standard scale in case of a vehicle adapted to carry more than eight passengers (b) Level 3 on the standard scale in any other case			
Regulations under RTA section 49 made by virtue of section 51(2)	Contravention of requirement of regulations (which is declared by regulations to be an offence) that driver of goods vehicle being tested be present throughout test or drive, etc, vehicle as and when directed	Summarily	Level 3 on the standard scale			

RTA section 53(1)	Using, etc, goods vehicle without required plating certificate being in force	Summarily	Level 3 on the standard scale
RTA section 53(2)	Using, etc, goods vehicle without required goods vehicle test certificate being in force	Summarily	Level 4 on the standard scale
RTA section 53(3)	Using, etc, goods vehicle where Secretary of State is required by regulations under section 49 to be notified of an alteration to the vehicle or its equipment but has not been notified	Summarily	Level 3 on the standard scale
Regulations under RTA section 61 made by virtue of sub-section (4)	Contravention of requirement of regulations (which is declared by regulations to be an offence) that driver of goods vehicle being tested after alteration be present throughout test and drive, etc, vehicle as when directed	Summarily	Level 3 on the standard scale
RTA section 63(1)	Using, etc, goods vehicle without required certificate being in force showing that it complies with type approval requirements applicable to it	Summarily	Level 4 on the standard scale
RTA section 63(2)	Using, etc, certain goods vehicles for drawing trailer when plating certificate does not specify maximum laden weight for vehicle and trailer	Summarily	Level 3 on the standard scale

(1) Provision creating offence	(2) General nature of offence	(3) Mode of prosecution	(4) Punishment	(5) Disqualification	(6) Endorsement	(7) Penalty points
RTA section 63(3)	Using, etc, goods vehicle where Secretary of State is required to be notified under section 59 of alteration to it or its equipment but has not been notified	Summarily	Level 3 on the standard scale			
RTA section 64	Using goods vehicle with unauthorised weights as well as authorised weights marked on it	Summarily	Level 3 on the standard scale			
RTA section 64A	Failure to hold EC certificate of conformity for unregistered light passenger vehicle or motor cycle	Summarily	Level 3 on the standard scale			
RTA section 65	Supplying vehicle or vehicle part without required certificate being in force showing that it complies with type approval requirements applicable to it	Summarily	Level 5 on the standard scale			
RTA section 65A	Light passenger vehicles and motor cycles not to be sold without EC certificate of conformity	Summarily	Level 5 on the standard scale			
RTA section 67	Obstructing testing of vehicle by examiner on road or failing to comply with requirements of RTA section 67 or Schedule 2	Summarily	Level 3 on the standard scale			
RTA section 68	Obstructing inspection, etc, of . . . vehicle by examiner or failing to comply with requirement to take . . . vehicle for inspection	Summarily	Level 3 on the standard scale			

RTA section 71	Driving, etc, . . . vehicle in contravention of prohibition on driving it as being unfit for service, or refusing, neglecting or otherwise failing to comply with direction to remove a . . . vehicle found over-loaded	Summarily	Level 5 on the standard scale
RTA section 74	Contravention of regulations requiring goods vehicle operator to inspect, and keep records of inspection of, goods vehicles	Summarily	Level 3 on the standard scale
RTA section 75	Selling, etc, unroadworthy vehicle or trailer so as to make it unroadworthy	Summarily	Level 5 on the standard scale
RTA section 76(1)	Fitting of defective or unsuitable vehicle parts	Summarily	Level 5 on the standard scale
RTA section 76(3)	Supplying defective or unsuitable vehicle parts	Summarily	Level 4 on the standard scale
RTA section 76(8)	Obstructing examiner testing vehicles to ascertain whether defective or unsuitable part has been fitted, etc	Summarily	Level 3 on the standard scale
RTA section 77	Obstructing examiner testing condition of used vehicles at sale rooms, etc	Summarily	Level 3 on the standard scale
RTA section 78	Failing to comply with requirement about weighing motor vehicle or obstructing authorised person	Summarily	Level 5 on the standard scale

(1) Provision creating offence	(2) General nature of offence	(3) Mode of prosecution	(4) Punishment	(5) Disqualification	(6) Endorsement	(7) Penalty points
RTA section 81	Selling, etc, pedal cycle in contravention of regulations as to brakes, bells, etc	Summarily	Level 3 on the standard scale			
RTA section 83	Selling, etc, wrongly made tail lamps or reflectors	Summarily	Level 5 on the standard scale			
RTA section 87(1)	Driving otherwise than in accordance with a licence	Summarily	Level 3 on the standard scale	Discretionary in a case where the offender's driving would not have been in accordance with any licence that could have been granted to him	Obligatory in the case mentioned in column 5	3–6
RTA section 87(2)	Causing or permitting a person to drive [otherwise than in accordance with] a licence	Summarily	Level 3 on the standard scale			
RTA section 92(7C)	Failure to deliver licence revoked by virtue of section 92(7A) and counterpart to Secretary of State	Summarily	Level 3 on the standard scale			
RTA section 92(10)	Driving after making false declaration as to physical fitness	Summarily	Level 4 on the standard scale	Discretionary	Obligatory	3–6
RTA section 93(3)	Failure to deliver revoked licence and counterpart to Secretary of State	Summarily	Level 3 on the standard scale			

RTA section 94(3) and that sub-section as applied by RTA section 99D or 109C	Failure to notify Secretary of State of onset of, or deterioration in, relevant or prospective disability	Summarily	Level 3 on the standard scale			
RTA section 94(3A) and that sub-section as applied by RTA section 99D(b) or 109C(c)	Driving after such a failure	Summarily	Level 3 on the standard scale	Discretionary	Obligatory	3–6
RTA section 94A	Driving after refusal of licence under section 92(3), revocation under section 93 or service of a notice under section 99C or 109B	Summarily	6 months or level 5 on the standard scale or both	Discretionary	Obligatory	3–6
RTA section 96	Driving with uncorrected defective eyesight, or refusing to submit to test of eyesight	Summarily	Level 3 on the standard scale	Discretionary	Obligatory	3
RTA section 99(5)	Driving licence holder failing to surrender licence and counterpart	Summarily	Level 3 on the standard scale			
RTA section 99B(11) and that subsection as applied by RTA section 109A(5)	Driving after failure to comply with a requirement under section 99B(6), (7) or (10) or a requirement under section 99B(6) or (7) as applied by section 109A(5)	Summarily	Level 3 on the standard scale			
RTA section 99C(4)	Failure to deliver Community licence to Secretary of State when required by notice under section 99C	summarily	Level 3 on the standard scale			
RTA section 103(1)(a)	Obtaining driving licence while disqualified	Summarily	Level 3 on the standard scale			

(1) Provision creating offence	(2) General nature of offence	(3) Mode of prosecution	(4) Punishment	(5) Disqualification	(6) Endorsement	(7) Penalty points
RTA 103(1)(b)	Driving while disqualified	(a) Summarily, in England and Wales	(a) 6 months or level 5 on the standard scale or both	Discretionary	Obligatory	6
		(b) Summarily, in Scotland	(b) 6 months or the statutory maximum or both			
		(c) On indictment, in Scotland	(c) 12 months or a fine or both			
RTA section 109	...	Summarily	Level 3 on the standard scale			
RTA section 109B(4)	Failure to deliver Northern Ireland licence to Secretary of State when required by notice under section 109B					
...	...	...	...			
RTA section 114	Failing to comply with conditions of LGV PCV licence or LGV Community licence, or causing or permitting person under 21 to drive LGV or PCV in contravention of such conditions	Summarily	Level 3 on the standard scale			
RTA section 115A(4)	Failure to deliver LGV or PCV Community licence when required by notice under section 115A	Summarily	Level 3 on the standard scale			
RTA section 118	Failing to surrender revoked or suspended LGV or PCV licence and counterpart	Summarily	Level 3 on the standard scale			
Regulations made by virtue of RTA section 120(5)	Contravention of provision of regulations (which is declared by regulations to be an offence) about LGV or PCV driver's licences or LGV or PCV Community licence	Summarily	Level 3 on the standard scale			

RTA section 123(4)	Giving of paid driving instruction by unregistered and unlicensed persons or their employers	Summarily	Level 4 on the standard scale
RTA section 123(6)	Giving of paid instruction without there being exhibited on the motor car a certificate of registration or a licence under RTA Part V	Summarily	Level 3 on the standard scale
RTA section 125A(4)	Failure, on application for registration as disabled driving instructor, to notify Registrar of onset of, or deterioration in, relevant or prospective disability	Summarily	Level 3 on the standard scale
RTA section 133C(4)	Failure by registered or licensed disabled driving instructor to notify Registrar of onset of, or deterioration in, relevant or prospective disability	Summarily	Level 3 on the standard scale
RTA section 133D	Giving of paid driving instruction by disabled persons or their employers without emergency control certificate or in un-authorised motor car	Summarily	Level 3 on the standard scale
RTA section 135	Unregistered instructor using title or displaying badge, etc, prescribed for registered instructor, or employer using such title, etc, in relation to his unregistered instructor or issuing misleading advertisement, etc	Summarily	Level 4 on the standard scale

(1) Provision creating offence	(2) General nature of offence	(3) Mode of prosecution	(4) Punishment	(5) Disqualification	(6) Endorsement	(7) Penalty points
RTA section 136	Failure of instructor to surrender to Registrar certificate or licence	Summarily	Level 3 on the standard scale			
RTA section 137	Failing to produce certificate of registration or licence as driving instructor	Summarily	Level 3 on the standard scale			
RTA section 143	Using motor vehicle while uninsured or unsecured or against third party risks	Summarily	Level 5 on the standard scale	Discretionary	Obligatory	6–8
RTA section 147	Failing to surrender certificate of insurance or security to insurer on cancellation or to make statutory declaration of loss or destruction	Summarily	Level 3 on the standard scale			
RTA section 154	Failing to give information, or wilfully making a false statement, as to insurance or security when claim made	Summarily	Level 4 on the standard scale			
RTA section 163	Failing to stop [mechanically propelled] vehicle or cycle when required by constable	Summarily	(a) Level 5 on the standard scale if committed by a person driving a mechanically propelled vehicle. (b) Level 3 on the standard scale if committed by a person riding a cycle.			
RTA section 164	Failing to produce driving licence or counterpart etc or to state date of birth, or failing to provide the Secretary of State with evidence of date of birth, etc	Summarily	Level 3 on the standard scale			

Provision	General nature of offence	Mode of prosecution	Punishment	Disqualification	Endorsement	Penalty points
RTA section 165	Failing to give . . . certain names and addresses or to produce certain documents	Summarily	Level 3 on the standard scale			
RTA section 168	Refusing to give, or giving false, name and address in case of reckless, careless or inconsiderate driving or cycling	Summarily	Level 3 on the standard scale			
RTA section 169	Pedestrian failing to give constable his name and address after failing to stop when directed by constable controlling traffic	Summarily	Level 1 on the standard scale			
RTA section 170(4)	Failing to stop after accident and give particulars or report accident	Summarily	Six months or level 5 on the standard scale or both	Discretionary	Obligatory	5–10
RTA section 170(7)	Failure by driver, in case of accident involving injury to another, to produce evidence of insurance or security or to report accident	Summarily	Level 3 on the standard scale			
RTA section 171	Failure by owner of motor vehicle to give police information for verifying compliance with requirement of compulsory insurance or security	Summarily	Level 4 on the standard scale			
RTA section 172	Failure of person keeping vehicle and others to give police information as to identity of driver, etc, in the case of certain offences	Summarily	Level 3 on the standard scale	Discretionary, if committed otherwise than by virtue of subsection (5) or (11)	Obligatory, if committed otherwise than by virtue of subsection (5) or (11)	6

(1) Provision creating offence	(2) General nature of offence	(3) Mode of prosecution	(4) Punishment	(5) Disqualification	(6) Endorsement	(7) Penalty points
RTA section 173	Forgery etc, of licences, counterparts of Community licences, test certificates, certificates of insurance and other documents and things	(a) Summarily (b) On indictment	(a) The statutory maximum (b) 2 years			
RTA section 174	Making certain false statements, etc, and withholding certain material information	(a) Summarily (b) On indictment	(a) 6 months or the statutory maximum or both (b) 2 years or a fine or both			
RTA section 175 175(1) 175(2)	Issuing false documents Falsely amending certificate of conformity	Summarily Summarily	Level 4 on the standard scale Level 4 on the standard scale			
RTA section 177	Impersonation of, or of person employed by, authorised examiner	Summarily	Level 3 on the standard scale			
RTA section 178	Taking, etc, in Scotland a motor vehicle without authority or, knowing that it has been so taken, driving it or allowing oneself to be carried in it without authority	(a) Summarily (b) On indictment	(a) 3 months or the statutory maximum or both (b) 12 months or a fine or both	Discretionary	...	...
RTA section 180	Failing to attend, give evidence or produce documents to, inquiry held by Secretary of State, etc	Summarily	Level 3 on the standard scale			
RTA section 181	Obstructing inspection of vehicles after accident	Summarily	Level 3 on the standard scale			
RTA Schedule 1 paragraph 6	Applying warranty to equipment, protective helmet, appliance or information in defending proceedings under RTA section 15A, 17 or 18(4) where no warranty given, or applying false warranty	Summarily	Level 3 on the standard scale			

Offences under this Act

Section 25 of this Act	Failing to give information as to date of birth or sex to court or to provide Secretary of State with evidence of date of birth, etc	Summarily	Level 3 on the standard scale
Section 26 of this Act	Failing to produce driving licence and counterpart to court making order for interim disqualification . . .	Summarily	Level 3 on the standard scale
Section 27 of this Act	Failing to produce licence and counterpart to court for endorsement on conviction of offence involving obligatory endorsement or on committal for sentence, etc, for offence involving obligatory or discretionary disqualification when no interim disqualification ordered	Summarily	Level 3 on the standard scale
Section 62 of this Act	Removing fixed penalty notice fixed to vehicle	Summarily	Level 2 on the standard scale
Section 67 of this Act	False statement in response to notice to owner	Summarily	Level 5 on the standard scale

SCHEDULE 3—FIXED PENALTY OFFENCES

Section 51

(1) **Provision creating offence**	(2) **General nature of offence**
Offence under the Greater London Council (General Powers) Act 1974 (c xxiv)	
Section 15 of the Greater London Council (General Powers) Act 1974.	Parking vehicles on footways, verges, etc.
Offence under the Highways Act 1980 (c 60)	
Section 137 of the Highways Act 1980.	Obstructing a highway, but only where the offence is committed in respect of a vehicle.
Offences under the Road Traffic Regulation Act 1984 (c 27)	
RTRA section 5(1)	Using a vehicle in contravention of a traffic regulation order outside Greater London.
RTRA section 8(1)	Breach of traffic regulation order in Greater London.
RTRA section 11	Breach of experimental traffic order.
RTRA section 13	Breach of experimental traffic scheme regulations in Greater London.
RTRA section 16(1)	Using a vehicle in contravention of temporary prohibition or restriction of traffic in case of execution of works, etc.
RTRA section 17(4)	Wrongful use of special road.
RTRA section 18(3)	Using a vehicle in contravention of provision for one-way traffic on trunk road.
RTRA section 20(5)	Driving a vehicle in contravention of order prohibiting or restricting driving vehicles on certain classes of roads.
RTRA section 25(5)	Breach of pedestrian crossing regulations, except an offence in respect of a moving motor vehicle other than a contravention of regulations 23, 24, 25 and 26 of the Zebra, Pelican and Puffin Pedestrian Crossings Regulations and General Directions 1997.

(1) **Provision creating offence**	(2) **General nature of offence**
RTRA section 29(3)	Using a vehicle in contravention of a street playground order . . .
RTRA section 35A(1)	Breach of an order regulating the use, etc, of a parking place provided by a local authority, but only where the offence is committed in relation to a parking place provided on a road.
RTRA section 47(1)	Breach of a provision of a parking place designation order and other offences committed in relation to a parking place designated by such an order, except any offence of failing to pay an excess charge within the meaning of section 46.
RTRA section 53(5)	Using vehicle in contravention of any provision of a parking place designation order having effect by virtue of section 53(1)(a) (inclusion of certain traffic regulation provisions).
RTRA section 53(6)	Breach of a provision of a parking place designation order having effect by virtue of section 53(1)(b) (use of any part of a road for parking without charge).
RTRA section 88(7)	Driving a motor vehicle in contravention of an order imposing a minimum speed limit under section 88(1)(b)
RTRA section 89(1)	Speeding offences under RTRA and other Acts.

Offences under the Road Traffic Act 1988 (c 52)

RTA section 14	Breach of regulations requiring wearing of seat belts.
RTA section 15(2)	Breach of restriction on carrying children in the front of vehicles.
RTA section 15(4)	Breach of restriction on carrying children in the rear of vehicles.
RTA section 16	Breach of regulations relating to protective headgear for motor cycle drivers and passengers.
RTA section 18(3)	Breach of regulations relating to head-worn appliances (eye protectors) for use on motor cycles.
RTA section 19	Parking a heavy commercial vehicle on verge or footway.
RTA section 22	Leaving vehicle in dangerous position.
RTA section 23	Unlawful carrying of passengers on motor cycles.
RTA section 24	Carrying more than one person on a pedal cycle.
RTA section 34	Driving motor mechanically propelled vehicle elsewhere than on a road.
RTA section 35	Failure to comply with traffic directions.
RTA section 36	Failure to comply with traffic signs.

(1) **Provision creating offence**	(2) **General nature of offence**
RTA section 40A	Using vehicle in dangerous condition etc.
RTA section 41A	Breach of requirement as to brakes, steering-gear or tyres.
RTA section 41B	Breach of requirement as to weight: goods and passenger vehicles.
RTA section 41D	Breach of requirement as to control of vehicle, mobile telephone etc.
RTA section 42	[Breach of other construction and use requirements.
RTA section 47	Using, etc, vehicle without required test certificate being in force].
RTA section 87(1)	Driving vehicle otherwise than in accordance with requisite licence.
RTA section 143	Using motor vehicle while uninsured or unsecured against third party risks.
RTA section 163	Failure to stop vehicle on being so required by constable in uniform.
RTA section 172	Failure of person keeping vehicle and others to give the police information as to identity of driver, etc, in the case of certain offences.

Offences under the Vehicle Excise and Registration Act 1994 (c 22)

Section 33 of the Vehicle Excise and Registration Act 1994	Using or keeping a vehicle on a public road without vehicle licence, trade licence or nil licence being exhibited in manner prescribed by regulations.
Section 42 of that Act	Driving or keeping a vehicle without required registration mark.
Section 43 of that Act	Driving or keeping a vehicle with registration mark obscured etc.
Section 43C of that Act	Using an incorrectly registered vehicle.
Section 59 of that Act	Failure to fix prescribed registration mark to a vehicle in accordance with regulations made under section 23(4)(a) of that Act.

Offences under the Highways Act 1835 and the Roads (Scotland) Act 1984

Section 72 of the Highways Act 1835	Driving on the footway.
	Cycling on the footway.
Section 129(5) of the Roads (Scotland) Act 1984	Driving on the footway.

Appendix 3

Drink/Driving—Alcohol Concentrations and Table of Metabolic Losses for Breath and Blood Analyses with Time

ALCOHOL CONCENTRATIONS

Conversion of breath-alcohol (μg/100ml) to blood/urine-alcohol (mg/100ml)

Alcohol/ Breath	Alcohol/ Alcohol/Blood	Urine	Breath	Blood	Urine
26	60	80	83	190	254
27	62	83	85	195	260
28	64	86	87	200	267
29	67	89	89	205	274
30	69	92	91	210	280
31	71	95	94	215	287
32	74	98	96	220	294
33	76	101	98	225	300
34	78	104	100	230	307
35	80	107	102	235	314
37	85	113	105	240	321
39	90	120	107	245	327
41	95	127	109	250	334
43	100	133	111	255	347
45	105	140	113	260	341
48	110	147	115	265	354
50	115	153	118	270	361
52	120	160	120	275	367
54	125	167	122	280	374
56	130	173	65	150	200
59	135	180	67	155	207
61	140	187	70	160	214
63	145	193	72	165	220
74	170	227	124	285	381
76	175	234	126	290	387
78	180	240	129	295	394
80	185	247	131	300	401

To convert breath-alcohol readings outside of these figures, multiply breath-alcohol result by 2.3 and round to the nearest whole number to obtain the equivalent blood-alcohol reading; multiply by 3.06 for urine-alcohol reading.

TABLE OF METABOLIC LOSSES FOR BREATH AND BLOOD ANALYSES WITH TIME

Breath (μg%) Blood (mg%)	15min	30min	45min	60min	75min	90min
35	33	31	30	28	26	25
80	76	72	68	65	61	57
40	38	36	35	33	31	30
92	88	84	80	77	73	69
45	43	41	40	38	36	35
103	99	95	91	88	84	80
50	48	46	45	43	41	40
115	111	107	103	100	96	92
55	53	51	50	48	46	45
126	122	118	114	111	107	103
60	58	56	55	53	51	50
138	134	130	126	123	119	115
65	63	61	60	58	56	55
149	145	141	137	137	130	126
70	68	66	65	63	61	60
161	157	153	149	146	142	138
75	73	71	70	68	66	65
172	168	164	160	157	153	149
80	78	76	75	73	71	70
184	130	176	172	169	165	161
85	83	81	80	78	76	75
195	191	187	183	180	176	172
90	88	86	85	83	81	80
207	203	199	195	192	188	184
95	93	91	90	88	86	85
218	214	210	206	203	199	195
100	98	96	95	93	91	90
230	226	222	218	215	211	207
105	103	101	100	98	96	95
241	237	233	229	226	222	218
10	108	106	105	103	101	100
253	249	245	241	238	234	230
115	113	111	10	108	106	105
264	260	256	252	249	245	241
120	18	116	115	13	111	110
276	272	268	264	261	257	253
125	123	121	120	118	116	115
287	283	279	275	272	268	264
130	128	126	125	123	121	120

Index